FIND THE LOVE OF YOUR LIFE AFTER FIFTY!

Alice Solomon

The Writers' Collective   Cranston, Rhode Island

Independent books for Independent Readers

Printed in the United States of America
10 11 10 09 08 07 06 05 04 03   5 4 3 2 1

ISBN: 1-932133-68-2

book design by MyLinda Butterworth
cover design by Samantha Wall

Library of Congress Cataloging-in-Publication Data
Solomon, Alice, 1934-
  Find the love of your life after fifty! / by Alice Solomon.
      p. cm.
Includes bibliographical references (p.) and index.
  ISBN 1-932133-68-2 (TP : alk. paper)
  1. Dating (Social customs) 2. Middle aged women—Psychology. 3. Man-woman relationships. I. Title.
  HQ801.S665 2003
  646.7'7'0844—dc21

                              2003004268

Published by The Writers' Collective
Cranston, Rhode Island

A NO-NONSENSE SURVEY OF WHAT MAKES DATING AFTER 50 DIFFERENT Find The Love Of Your Life After 50! by Alice Solomon is an invaluable and thoroughly "user friendly" self-help guide to the singles scene for women over fifty. From the advantages of computer dating; to a no-nonsense survey of what makes dating after 50 different; to the type of man one is most compatible with; to where to meet single men who would have an interest in older women, and so much more, Find The Love Of Your Life After 50! is an excellent primer embodying both the romantic and the practical.

Midwest Book Review
***** Amazon.com

"In France, men adore "femmes d'une certaine age." Alice shows us how to be just as sexy and smart as the Parisan "women of a certain age!"
- Leil Lowndes, author, How to Make Anyone Fall in Love with You

"Memo to members of the 50-plus single female crowd who have bought into the "I'm doomed to live alone" doldrums: Snap out of it! Read Alice Solomon's Find the Love of Your Life After 50! and stop schlepping to the market and the dry cleaners when you should be strutting! Coyness is out. Defeatism, picky-picky and long-suffering patience - ditto. Solomon, who has spent years in the grandma dating trenches, knows the terrain, the tactics and the enemy: those dumb catch-me-if-you- can attitudes that might have worked in 1957.
It's 2003 and Find the Love of Your Life After 50! explains that Glamorous Grandmas - the vivacious women over 50 who love men and will settle for nothing less than to be loved back - can find love within the year. But only if they suit up and re-introduce themselves to the world of eligible men with verve, confidence and yes, glamour."
- Ron Wiggins, Columnist, the Palm Beach Post

"Alice Solomon is a trailblazer for women of all ages. She is not afraid to speak out about competing as an older woman in the business world or how to find love after fifty. Women of all ages can benefit from her experiences."
- Kelli Kennedy, Staff Writer, Boca Raton News

"Alice Solomon is a real inspiration for those meeting the dating scene head-on after the big Five-O."
- Peggy Austen, Editor, Aging with Style Magazine

"Alice's zest for life is contagious. She's embedded with the single senior culture and speaks from the heart. Her new book is must-read for any single woman, regardless of age."
- Jennifer London, Emmy Award Winning Journalist.

THIS BOOK IS FOR WOMEN OF ANY AGE Don't let the title of the book fool you: FIND THE LOVE OF YOUR LIFE AFTER 50! This book is for women of any age, and for men as well, if they'd like some insight into the female mind and heart. For the younger set, the whole idea of the book may seem silly…but life does NOT end at thirty…and women and men in the fifth, sixth, seventh, and eighth decades of their lives have emotional and sexual needs as do their younger counterparts.

Alice Solomon has written a very sensible and insightful book about a long-ignored sector of the dating population. In this book written to and for "Gorgeous Grandmas," Solomon addresses issues such as how dating and relationships differ at this life stage than in younger years. Skin care is discussed as well as the importance of good grooming, and makeup for the mid-life woman. Realistic and varied places are presented for consideration of meeting new people, as well as prompts to remain open-minded and non-judgmental when doing so.

Because people who are meeting one another at this point in their lives are not looking to marry in order to raise a family, it is pointed out that readers should reflect on what lifestyle changes they are willing to make…and those that they are not. There are multiple self-help quizzes to aid the reader in her quest to make the most of this portion of her dating life.

Alice Solomon writes from personal experience, as well as that of her friends and readers and listeners to both her formerly syndicated newspaper column and as a former radio show co-host. The book is written in a clear and flowing style, easy-to-read and unpretentious. Reading FINDING THE LOVE OF YOUR LIFE AFTER 50! is like having great conversations with a good friend.

Deb Jones, Online Book Reviewer
*****BN.com
Barnes and Noble

*This book is dedicated to
to my Significant Other,
Dan Levitan.*

*The Gorgeous Grandma endeavors —
newspaper columns, books,
Web site, radio shows,
and seminars —
would not have blossomed or thrived
without his encouragement
and support.*

TABLE OF CONTENTS

ACKNOWLEDGEMENTS

The concept of Gorgeous Grandma began in the office of Marcie Schorr Hirsch, former director of external programs at Wellesley College. Marcie's enthusiasm and encouragement thrust many GGs into new and wonderful careers as well as fruitful, rewarding endeavors. I shall be indebted always to Marcie and her husband, Ralph Hirsch, for their kindnesses on my behalf.

My good friend, Virginia Lucier, a well-known reporter for the *Middlesex News* in Framingham, Massachusetts, was largely responsible for introducing to the newspaper my monthly column "A Guide For Gorgeous Grandmas." A very appreciative thank you, Virginia, for your assistance and encouragement.

My former editors at the *Middlesex News,* Karen Buckley, Carol Beggy, and Rodney Schussler, have also been important to the success of "A Guide For Gorgeous Grandmas." Without their acceptance, the column would have been history for sure. Thank you very much for the opportunities you offered to me and to our readers.

Along with the former editor in chief of the *MetroWest Daily News*, Andrea Haynes, and the current editor in chief, Russ Lodi, to whom I am most grateful, I would like to thank my colleagues, Bob Tremblay and Naomi Kodeer, for their editing expertise. Also, to Sandy Buentello, our librarian, a warm thank you for your assistance.

Those newspaper columns, which inspired my books, could not have lived their lovely, long life without our wonderful readers, who shared their ideas and stories with me in their letters, in conversations, during personal appearances, and via e-mail. I want to thank you all for your enthusiasm, your input, and your interest over the years. Too, a big hug to all the wonderful clubs and organizations who have invited me to speak in southern Florida.

To book editor, Carrie Cantor, bookcover designer, Samantha Wall, book designer, MyLinda Butterworth, book indexer, Dan Connolly, and especially to Lisa Grant of the Writers Collective, a warm and heartfelt thank you. Your combined talents and skills contributed enormously to the success of this project.

To my proofreaders and good friends, Rhoda Cahan, Nancy Greenfield, and Evelyn Gluckstern, a warm appreciation for your time and efforts on my behalf. To Francine Schwartz, a special friend, my sincere appreciation for your professionalism, companionship, and interest as you accompany me to seminars and speaking engagements. To Dar McDermott, my talented golf buddy, a big hug to you for your photographic expertise.

To my loving family - dear sons, James and Harold, dear daughters-in-law, Karen and Nancy, and my five beautiful grandchildren - Sarah, Benjamin, Alec, Isabel, and Nicholas - I am deeply grateful for the years of love and great joy you have brought into my life. And I am so happy to welcome dear Matt Levitan and his lovely bride, Jessica, to our loving family.

To my dear friends, especially Letty Zieman, who have observed and shared with me the comical, bizarre, and often curious adventures of singlehood, I am especially thankful for your friendship, the stability you keep bringing to my life, and the sense of humor you continue to exhibit.

Last, but never the least, to dear Dan Levitan - who has been the special person in my life for the last seven years - I wish to offer my love, gratitude, and appreciation for your love, respect, companionship, and patience. I cherish having you by my side except, at times, on the golf course.

INTRODUCTION

ROMANCE FOR GORGEOUS GRANDMAS

Finding romance at a later stage in life can be incredibly elusive. When a single woman over fifty, who bring many years of life experience with her, ventures out to seek a companion for pleasurable years ahead, she faces a changed and unfamiliar social world. In fact, with fewer unattached men to be found as a woman ages, it becomes more and more difficult for her to know how and where to meet men.

We hear often from gals in their late twenties, thirties, and forties that being single isn't fun, but it is a far more common complaint of single women over fifty, particularly if they have been married before and had a loving, or even a less-than-loving relationship, with their husbands. In fact, most of these women say that being one half of a couple again would be wonderful, especially since couplehood is the preferred way to socialize among the over-fifty crowd.

Hence, a dilemma. What do they do? How do they go about finding companionship? Where can they meet that special person? Are there secrets to finding romance and companionship in later life?

Hello, and welcome to the world of Gorgeous Grandmas. It will be my pleasure, on the following pages, to share with you what I have learned through research, experience, interaction with readers of my newspaper columns, and during speaking engagements before numerous single women's groups, on venturing out into the single world and experiencing the lumps and bumps of dating after fifty.

But first, who is a Gorgeous Grandma, you might ask?

The concept of Gorgeous Grandma began following my graduation from college at age fifty. I returned to the real world to discover that many worldly observers were ignoring our generation and especially the single women in it.

Our crowd - those who attended high school and college in the late 1940s, '50s, and early '60s - were, and are, a relatively sane, stable group. As a result, we weren't noteworthy enough to be studied, written about, criticized, or even celebrated very much. Only over the last few years has the media and advertising crowd begun to notice that we are here and that many of us are affluent, powerful, and conspicuous.

Meanwhile, experiences in public relations, marketing, and fashion kept me in touch with hundreds of women, and numerous opportunities arose for me to observe my peers closely. To my dismay, I discovered that many gals over fifty (and men too) had begun to lose their enthusiasm, their joie de vivre, and their motivation for a good life because "it's almost too late to try anymore."

In response to that, I began writing a newspaper column in 1994 for the *MetroWest Daily News* in Framingham, Massachusetts, and other newspapers in Massachusetts and Florida, focusing on women of my generation who had a lust for life but needed more than a boost to get from just surviving to thriving. Indeed, we all have a lot more living to do, regardless of age.

For months, I tried to think of a name for our group, one that would be upbeat, catchy, and grab attention. Finally, "Gorgeous" was selected because it presents a snappy "notice me" image, while "Grandma" instantly defines an age group and stage of life, regardless of whether a woman is actually a grandmother.

Hence, Gorgeous Grandma is not meant to be taken literally. It is meant to make us smile and take notice. And isn't a smile and some attention a good beginning?

After the newspaper column appeared, I began to receive wonderful feedback from our many readers. Fifteen months later, "A Guide for Gorgeous Grandmas" was being published weekly, biweekly, or monthly in thirteen newspapers, with a circulation of over 150,000 readers. I wrote often about the dilemmas of single life.

Who is a Gorgeous Grandma? She is every woman over fifty who:

* Believes she has her whole life ahead of her, not just behind her.

* Wants to get the most out of every day of her life.

* Wants to thrive, not just survive.

* Cares for her mind and her body.

* Remains adaptable to life's bittersweet as well as its sweet.

* Cherishes herself as much as she cherishes her loved ones.

* Refuses to remain static and is, instead, always open to learning, new ideas, new challenges, and new experiences.

* Loves life - and let's everyone know it!

It is my sincere hope that this book will, in some way, encourage and motivate you, dear reader, to renew, refresh, and revitalize life by seeking again a fine man to share it with.

What then does it take to find a mate, a buddy, a pal, a companion, a lover, at this stage in life?

* It takes the recognition that dating is different from years past.

* It takes courage.

* It takes the right timing.

* It takes being adaptable.

* It takes being realistic, creative, and educating yourself.

* It takes looking good.

* It takes avoiding married men.

* And, at the very least, it takes knowing the best places to meet men.

What a task, you might say.

Not really. It's easier than you think.

Join me as we explore how to bring romance into your life once more and find the love of your life after fifty!

1

DATING IS DIFFERENT AT THIS AGE

*Wouldn't it be wonderful if those who bothered us
when we were young and busy would come
back when we are old and lonely?*

Lois was frustrated about her recent blind date: "I met him at a local spot, we had a drink or two, and we danced for a while. He was quite pleasant and I haven't been out with a guy in so long, it was just nice being in his company. Because I had made brownies that afternoon and I thought he might like them, I invited him home to have coffee. I was so used to having people back to the house while I was married, that I didn't think twice about inviting Phil to do the same. However, as he was leaving to go home, Phil told me he had learned that when a woman invites a man in 'for coffee,' it means that she wants to go to bed with him. I wanted to kick him out the door."

Lois is not alone in her frustration. Dating has changed.

I'll never forget my first date when I decided to reenter the dating world. A friend called to ask if she could give my number to a fellow who had just divorced. He was "tall, handsome, very nice, and very successful."

How thoughtful of her, and why not?

David called me (his name is fictitious, as are all the names I use - in this case, to be more benevolent to the guilty than to protect the innocent) and he asked if I would like to drive to Provincetown, Massachusetts (two hours from my home) for a leisurely stroll and an early dinner. Foolishly, I agreed.

He came by at 1:00 in the afternoon. By 6:00, we were seated in a charming restaurant at a lovely table with candles and wine. We had spent a pleasant afternoon driving leisurely to Cape Cod and then walking around town talking.

After enjoying an appetizer and a few glasses of wine, he excused himself to go to the men's room. When he returned, he became angry at me (for what I believed to be no reason), which was as surprising as it was totally unacceptable. I asked to be driven home immediately. For two painfully long hours, he kept up his barrage, including comments about women in general and his former wife in particular.

I rolled myself tightly in my comforter that night, with self-pity working overtime. A few days later, I learned that on the morning of our date, he had received word about a disturbing settlement on his second divorce. Hence, he was far from ready to socialize with this sensitive creature or, in fact, any other woman. I resolved not to date so far from home again, except with someone I knew very well.

I would guess most of us single GGs have a story or two to tell, and I'll bet the fellows have just as many. It goes with the territory. Nonetheless, where we shall focus now is on what the newly widowed or divorced Gorgeous Grandma might expect when she ventures forth to begin socializing with men again at this stage of life.

Has dating changed that much from what we remember years ago? When I asked that question to my then-single twenty-something son, he answered that it was still the same, but, on the other hand, it was a lot different. Wondering why we paid all that money for his college education, I moved on to explore the unknown for myself.

What did I discover? He was right (forgive me, dear). Dating is the same, but it is different - a lot different from what you and I experienced before we were married.

Dating years ago, I remember us meeting fellows at college mixers, at fraternity parties, at dances. I remember us being fixed up by friends, friends of friends, and by friends of our parents. We had some connection with the men we dated. Very rarely were we in the company of a total stranger. Of course, most of us lived at home during those years, aside from our years at college. We were, for the most part, in a protected, nurturing, and supportive environment.

But, were we not expected to come home with a loving husband by the time college graduation rolled around or shortly thereafter? If college was not an option, many future Gorgeous Grandmas were married by the time they were sixteen or seventeen. In any case, we knew that we did not want to disappoint our parents by remaining single past the age of twenty-five. Establishing a family and bearing children was the expected future for the majority of us. Indeed, many of us submitted our total well-being into the hands of our husbands.

Our expectations now, regarding a man in our life? Quite a bit different than before, are they not? Our desire to seek and enter into a loving relationship grows out of fifty-plus years of experience at living. As mature, self-confident, wise, comfortable-in-our-own-skin women, we approach meeting and dating men with a different attitude. Indeed, our expectations and goals have changed.

The first consideration is whether a woman is *ready* to date again. When we were young and we broke up with a boyfriend, getting over that relationship, in most cases, lasted about as long as it took to find a new boyfriend. After many years of marriage, however, and after experiencing the painful loss of a loved one through death or divorce, it may take months and even years to recover. The healing process takes time. It is important to complete that process and feel good about oneself before beginning a new social life.

For the most part, the second time around, the focus of a relationship shifts away from child rearing to companionship, intimacy, sharing, and security. Now, most of us demonstrate an inclination to choose a companion, partner, or spouse on the basis of mutual interests plus the expected positives of good times, good laughs, love, and romance.

Another issue is that the thought of dating again can be scary and confusing. The possibility of being rejected makes it even worse. Let's face it: we have wrinkles; we have gained a little, if not a lot, of weight; we're too old to change, we think. We may be basically shy. Many widows say, "I took care of my sick husband for years before his death. I don't want to take care of another one." Too, it's not easy to anticipate a possible new relationship and perhaps another breakup. We question our ability to handle disappointment or rejection.

And then there's sex. For most of us, it's tough getting into bed with a stranger. Even if he was your former college sweetheart who has returned to you as a new beau or someone you've known for the last thirty years, he is still a stranger to your body. But, we are thankful to the women's movement of the '60s for changing society's view of women, and we are now quite free to determine our own standards for respectable sexual behavior rather than our mothers'.

But our body parts aren't working quite the same way they were when we were younger. And the sex drive, for most of our crowd, does diminish with age. Now, to counteract that testosterone slump, Viagra plays a large part in renewed sexual activity for our crowd which, in turn, leads to increased promiscuity for folks over fifty. H.I.V. and venereal disease are now growing fastest among people sixty-five and older. But you are aware of these facts, I'm sure, and and you know to take precautions when necessary.

Sex is still good, though, regardless of age. In fact, we are probably much less inhibited than when we were younger, and we might even teach the fellas something new!

Also, in the our younger years, when we were dating men, there were not yet any children to influence our decisions one way or another. Today, there might very well be grown-up children in the picture who have some influence on us. Perhaps there is a child or a grandchild who lives with us. It's difficult to find time (and sometimes energy) to start a new life. Perhaps our children do not care for the man we are dating. There might be misunderstandings or jealousies. For example:

> *Betsy, a widow at fifty-five, had just begun to socialize when she met an interesting doctor at a singles event one night. She was delighted to accept his invitation for a drink the following week.*
>
> *As Betsy was waiting for her date to arrive on the appointed evening, all was fine until her son, Eric, home on a college recess, reminded her that she had not finished his laundry. After Betsy left for the laundry room located down the hall, the doorman called and told Eric that Betsy's date had arrived and he was waiting in the lobby. When Betsy returned with Eric's laundry in hand, Eric said nothing. After Betsy had folded his clothes and placed them neatly back in his duffle, Eric informed his mother that the fellow was waiting.*
>
> *By the time Betsy threw on her coat, grabbed her pocketbook, kissed Eric goodbye, walked down the hall to the elevator, waited for the elevator to arrive, and rode down to the lobby, her date had lost patience and left. Throwing dignity to the wind, Betsy ran and caught up with him a few blocks later. They did have that drink, but she never heard from him again.*
>
> *Apparently, Betsy was ready to move on with her life but her son was not eager to let her. She did not allow this incident to deter her, however. Betsy was determined to enjoy dating and to continue taking risks. She also intended to have a long talk with her son about the changes in his life and hers, as well as about his new responsibilities.*

How do we balance our childrens' wishes with our own needs and feelings? Children are very important to us, but our new life is very important, too. We must learn that children do adapt once we communicate openly with them and make our feelings known.

Too, children may have property concerns when a parent discusses remarrying. Oftentimes, children resent the new bride (or groom) and can start a great deal of trouble unless satisfactory financial arrangements are finalized to the benefit of the children. Even that arrangement can be troublesome if the parent dies. A friend of mine entered litigation with her significant other's children over the house he left her in his will after he passed away. The children fought her vigorously, even though the bequeath to her was their father's wish.

Many people who reenter the dating arena after years of married life have ghosts or hidden agendas. I like to think that most people are honest about themselves, but, let's face it, oftentimes they're not. The secrets about a potential partner that we eventually uncover may be ones we can't live with. It pays to be cautious before forming a lasting bond. It's wise to take a longer time to form that bond than it did in our younger days.

When you do start dating again, consider these guidelines:

1. **Try to make new friends**. It is tremendously important to recognize that your former life is over. I am not suggesting that you forget your past and your friends. I am urging you you to form new friendships that suit your current single lifestyle so that you will have a *better* social life. I did a great disservice to myself by clinging to old friendships, hoping that the stability and the security of old friends would shelter me from the work it takes to find new ones. I was wrong. It took me an unusually long time to accept and be comfortable with a new lifestyle. Please don't let it happen to you.

2. **Ask for support.** We are not islands unto ourselves. Do not hesitate to call family, friends, clergy, a

former mentor, when you need support or encouragement. A small problem solved immediately is one less matter for you to deal with. Making decisions alone can be tough. It's okay to call your near-and-dears or a professional to help.

3. **Take small steps.** When you take small steps, you can avoid feeling fearful. Each morning, when awakening, think about new ways to move forward. Do something new every day. Buy new eyeglass frames. Start a journal. Just keep moving!

4. **Recognize the areas of life over which you have control.** When matters seem chaotic, take the time to think about the situation and seek an area you can control. You can't determine someone else's responses or reactions, but you can control your own. Find things you can make decisions about: whether or not to change your job or hair color, start a diet, take a trip. Starting small and getting control will enable you to gain confidence and reclaim power over other areas of your life.

~ QUIZ ~

Develop an Ageless Attitude

Because you are beginning a new and different social life, it might be fun to explore how you feel about aging. You may have not yet discovered that a truly positive attitude toward age can affect how well you feel and look, as well as how you come across to others.

From time to time, I am delighted by certain women whose attitude about age is so upbeat and infectious that they seem much younger than their years. Isn't it fun being around a person of any age, in fact, who has a great attitude?

There are many women who have a sadly negative attitude about age, even about aging well. Consequently, I thought it might be helpful to borrow a self-help questionnaire (adapted from *Longevity* magazine) to uncover and possibly improve your attitude about aging as you start out again in the single world.

How vital, energetic, enthusiastic, and sexy are you at this stage in your life? Do you feel wonderfully "ageless" or are you "old"? Begin by answering the following questions; then add up your score.

1. Do you think you look good?
    Very much (2) Somewhat (1) Not at all (0)

2. Do you admire people your age (and older) and think of them as productive and attractive?
    Very much (2) Somewhat (1) Not at all (0)

3.	How much have you changed your hairstyle in the last five years to look better or younger?
Very much (2) Somewhat (1) Not at all (0)

4.	Do your friends have positive attitudes toward aging?
Very much (2) Somewhat (1) Not at all (0)

5.	Do you feel old?
Very much (0)   Somewhat (1) Not at all (2)

6.	How much have you updated your wardrobe in the last five years?
Very much (2) Somewhat (1) Not at all (0)

7.	When you hit a major birthday (fifty-five, sixty, etc.), do you become depressed?
Very much (0) Somewhat (1) Not at all (2)

8.	Do the signs of aging you see on your face appear to you as attractive badges of experience?
Very much (2) Somewhat (1) Not at all (0)

9.	Do you think the physical signs of aging are bad?
Very much (0) Somewhat (1) Not at all (2)

10.	Have you made much effort in recent years to live a healthier lifestyle by cutting down on high-fat food and getting more exercise?
Very much (2) Somewhat (1) Not at all (0)

11.	Do you feel that looking older is a liability at work?
Very much (0) Somewhat (1) Not at all (2)

12. Do you feel that you are becoming less appealing sexually?
Very much (0) Somewhat (1) Not at all (2)

13. Do you feel satisfied with the life goals you've met so far?
Very much (2) Somewhat (1) Not at all (0)

14. Do you use cosmetics to look better?
Very much (2) Somewhat (1) Not at all (0)

15. Would you consider cosmetic surgery?
Very much (2) Somewhat (1) Not at all (0) (If you've already had it, give yourself 2 points.)

16. Have you changed your feelings about your appearance in the last ten years?
Very much (2) Somewhat (1) Not at all (0)

17. When you think of aging, do you think of an active sex life?
Very much (2) Somewhat (1) Not at all (0)

18. Does aging bring to mind maturity, valuable experience, wisdom, and the ability to contribute to society?
Very much (2) Somewhat (1) Not at all (0)

19. Do you continue to set new goals?
Very much (2) Somewhat (1) Not at all (0)

20. Do you feel hopeful, excited, or otherwise positive when you think ahead to the next ten years?
Very much (2) Somewhat (1) Not at all (0)

SCORING:

15-20: Congratulations! Your attitude is excellent. You will age gracefully and you will feel good and look good, no doubt, for many years to come.

8-14: Your aging attitude is about average. As with most people, you are bothered at times by wrinkles, gray hair, and your chronological age. Think about taking control over those areas of aging which are most troublesome to you. Perhaps a new hairstyle, fresh makeup, a new look would be more attractive for you. Improving your image can often divert attention (yours and others') away from chronological age and towards the ageless aspects of life: your intelligence, personality, talents, and friendship.

0-7: Oops, poor aging is obvious! It's time to shed that negativity about aging and take on a whole new attitude! Why not start by setting some goals for your relationships, appearance, and lifestyle. How about trying one new activity this week that will give you pleasure? And if your buddies tend to be "doom-and-gloom" types, seek out those who are more fun and upbeat.

Do remember that a truly positive attitude about aging will affect how well you feel, how good you look, and how charming you can be to the new men you will be bringing into your life.

2

GET OUT AND ABOUT TO MEET MEN

Too much of a good thing can be wonderful.
Mae West

Now that you've become more aware of how dating is different at this stage in life, let's move on to talk about *where to meet men*.

Where can you meet the love of your life? Almost anywhere. But, achieving this quest is totally up to you. The secret to success is *making up your mind* to put serious thought, time, and energy into finding him.

One evening, when I first became single, a girlfriend and I went to the theater. During intermission, on our way to the ladies room, my friend suggested we stand near the men's room in order to see if any interesting-looking fellows walked in or out. Dumb and undignified? Well, definitely undignified, but not so dumb.

Even though that type of thing may not be your style (or mine), it is still important to make an effort to bump into someone new accidentally or on purpose. Why should one do that? **Because reaching out to meet new people is the key to finding new relationships!** Those efforts might feel a little uncomfortable at first, but they soon become more comfortable in time.

Nonetheless, the best way to meet someone new is to be fixed up by a relative or friend. Why? Because the two of you will have a built-in common interest as well as far more trust than you would have if you met by chance. It is, then, in your best interest to mention, often, to your friends and family that you are interested in dating and that you would welcome recommendations should they run across anyone interesting.

I do confess I wish I'd had this advice in the early '80s when I first decided to return to the dating world. At that time, there weren't many people who understood where a single fifty-something was coming from. There were very few social clubs, singles groups, church or temple groups for singles over fifty, nor were there as many choices of acceptable places to meet men as there are now.

These days, fortunately, there are many singles groups, organizations, private clubs, and church/temple groups established as businesses or non-profit services that offer dances, coffees, teas, support groups, seminars, and travel opportunities exclusively for singles over fifty. They are terrific if you attend them with the right attitude: to have a pleasant time, a night out, and an opportunity to meet new people.

I do want to caution you against being disappointed if you don't find a new romance right away. More than likely you won't, and that may discourage you from attending further events. Please don't give up. There are plenty of people who have met their one and only through singles' clubs and organizations. And, do talk to other women who attend. You can meet some lovely new gal pals that way. Just pick up your local newspaper or your city's monthly magazine to find out where to go.

At any rate, let's begin to explore -

WHERE TO MEET MEN . . . BY CHANCE OR ON PURPOSE:

Local breakfast and lunch spots. Every city and town has at least one. Your task is to figure out where the nice fellows go.

On the streetcar, bus, train or plane. You never know where a chance meeting or conversation will lead. My son met his future wife on a train when he began a conversation with her girlfriend. Even I, who rarely talk to strangers, met a very nice fellow on the train to New York a while back. And, I started the conversation! (Actually, all I said was: "Is this seat taken?") Just a short while ago, I never would have ventured to say even that.

At the workplace. If you are a work horse, you get few opportunities to meet people outside the place where you spend most of your time. Then why not do some cultivating at work? Office romances are no longer frowned upon. And pay special attention to customers and/or clients. Even if they are not single, they most assuredly know men who are.

Business functions, trade shows, conventions. It's so nice to have a commonality of purpose to break the ice when business and travel coincide. If you're not in business, many major cities offer exhibits and trade shows open to the public. Why not choose an interest, grab a girlfriend, and go. Try a boat show, sports cars, home improvement, computers, antiques, food, flowers. In particular, I loved the flower show in Boston. It's in March every year, and what a lovely harbinger of spring.

Chambers of commerce and other professional organizations. These tend to meet on a regular basis. They offer great contacts and a common, relaxed meeting ground. These clubs are not only terrific for socializing, they also offer excellent opportunities for civic and community involvement. Because some clubs only opened their membership to women in the late 1980s, women constitute only 2 to 35 percent of club membership. Most club membership is by invitation only. It is best to contact the club of interest in your community and obtain an invitation to a meeting. The appendix to this book provides addresses and phone numbers of national headquarters for Kiwanis, Lions Clubs, and Rotary.

The following are suggestions for places to go or groups to join in order to pursue your interests and meet new people. The list is arranged according to areas of interest.

CULTURE

Bookstore events: Barnes & Noble and Borders bookstores offer lectures, book signings and even movies on a weekly basis, as well as a pleasing cafe environment. How charming it would be to meet a man over a book instead of over a drink for a change!

Theater groups: Many an amateur thespian has found romance behind the scenes! Look in your local phone book for information and in your community newspaper for tryouts. Even if you don't enjoy the footlights, behind the scenes can be lots of fun, and your talent for sewing, lighting, painting, or whatever will be of tremendous benefit to the troupe and the community.

Art galleries

Ballets

Choral societies

Festivals and fairs

Museums

Operas

Symphonies

All of the above are good places to begin conversations with members of the opposite sex. I know at least a few men who do the docent tours at our local museum, for example, and who meet any number of women in that manner. It's a fine way to meet someone with a mutual interest. At the very least, the fellow will most likely be cultured.

LEISURE ACTIVITIES

Antique cars
Backgammon
Bridge
Cat lovers' groups
Checkers
Chess
Coin collecting
Computers
Dinner lectures
Dog shows
Fishing
Flying
Folk dancing
Garden clubs

Investment clubs
Motorcycling
Photography clubs
Political organizations
Public speaking groups
Sailing
Scrabble
Sports car clubs
Square dancing
Stamp collecting
Vegetarian groups
Writers' clubs

SPORTS

Archery
Badminton
Ballooning
Bicycling
Bowling
Croquet
Curling
Diving
Fencing
Golf
Hiking
Horseshoes
Ice skating
Lifesaving
Polo
Paddle Tennis
River sports

Roller skating
Rowing
Running/Jogging
Skiing
Sledding
Softball
Squash/Racquetball
Swimming
Surfing
Table tennis
Tennis
Walking
Water skiing
Yacht racing
Yoga

Even if you do not wish to participate, why not go to watch a sport that you like? If you've not attended a sporting event in a while, it can be a refreshing change.

I happen to love walking along on the course watching pro golfers when the pro golf tour hits town. A while back, at the Seniors, a pleasant enough fellow, following the same foursome I was, began a conversation with me. I tend to find talking to strangers difficult and awkward, and so I didn't respond. But it was the perfect opportunity to meet someone new who shared one of my main interests. Wasn't I a dope!

(Please turn to Appendix F for contact information)

TRAVEL

Active Vacations
Bicycle tours   *Horseback riding*
Canoe trips   *Hostels*
Cattle drives and ranches   *Scuba diving*
Covered wagon trips   *Surfing*
Equestrian holidays   *White water rafting*
Farm vacations   *Wilderness trips*

Adventure Trips
American Wilderness Experience
Appalachian Mountain Club
Earthwatch
Outward Bound
Sierra Club

Please don't gasp when I suggest Outward Bound. If sixty-four-year-old Betty Friedan, author of *The Feminine Mystique* and *The Fountain of Age,* jogged three and a half miles every morning in mountain boots to prepare for her two-week-long wilderness survival with backpack, ran the rapids, climbed cliffs, refused to rappel a precipice, ran the risk of "being herself" and "going beyond"... why can't you?

In *The Fountain of Age*, Friedan reveals: "The young guides ... tell us how they dreaded taking on people as 'old' (55+) as we were purported to be. They figured we would hardly have the strength to paddle the rafts ourselves; they'd have to drag us through. They'd practiced CPR and emergency rescue drills and splints for our brittle, breakable bones. But, as it turns out, they didn't have to exert any extra effort, and we are the first group in years where no one has fallen overboard!"

(Please turn to Appendix G for contact information.)

Group Travel
Elderhostel
Eldertreks
Explorations in Travel
European Walking Tours
Family Hostel
Grandtravel
Saga Holidays
Seniors Abroad
Seniors At Sea

Travel businesses are focusing more and more on GGs, finally. We've all heard of Elderhostel and its concept and trips are terrific. But, if that doesn't fit the bill for you, there are any number of other organizations ready, willing, and able to satisfy your every whim, some of which I've listed here. There are also many alumni associations, museums, and zoos that offer tours suitable for older adults.

(Please turn to Appendix B for contact information).

Travel Companion and Travel for Singles Agencies
All Singles Travel
Discount Travel Club
O Solo Mio
Saga Holidays
Singles Travel International

Travel Companion Exchange
The Women's Travel Club

You who travel solo have all experienced the "single supplement" bite that most tour companies add when you choose to room alone. For seventeen years the Travel Companion Exchange has been building computerized lists to help single travelers find compatible companions. Members can specify that they'll travel only with a same-sex person or that they prefer the opposite sex. According to Jens Jurgen, the director of the service, more than 70 percent of his clients either request companions of the opposite sex or are willing to accept them; fewer than 15 percent want private rooms.

The Women's Travel Club offers its members a series of short or long trips each year. Shared or single accommodations are available, and men are invited to join some trips. Members receive a monthly newsletter, and local get-togethers are held.

Saga Holidays (mentioned under Group Travel as well) is a large tour operator that specializes in older travelers and has a few "singles only" departures. Saga also offers to find roommates for singles on cruises and tours.

O Solo Mio, All Singles Travel, Singles Travel International, and Discount Travel Club operate exclusively for singles. They offer anywhere from one tour a month to forty tours a year. The age range of travelers is from twenty through sixty. The ratio of men to women runs from 30 percent to 50 percent.

(Please see Appendix C and Appendix D for contact information)

Continuing Education

Adult education	*Home repair and*
Business seminars	*improvement courses*
Dale Carnegie training	*Language classes*
Dance instruction	*Music lessons*

Financial seminars   *Real estate seminars*
Gardening seminars   *Religious education*
Health seminars   *Sports lessons*
                             Tutoring

When an adult approaches furthering her education with a mature, interested, and enthusiastic mind set, a whole new world blossoms before her. Should you choose to undertake this formidable challenge on a degree-seeking level, your progress and ability will amaze you. There is so much to be gained, including new friends, new goals, a new career, achievements, insights, renewed self-esteem, greater confidence in your abilities, new interests, and, very possibly, that new man. But, first and foremost, you will be on the road to an amazing discovery - the discovery of yourself.

As for choosing a college to begin or continue your degree work, there are hundreds of fine institutions that welcome the nontraditional student (whom most colleges designate to be over the age of twenty-four). Attend some open-house forums of colleges close to your home in order to discuss programs, to meet the administration and faculty, to explore transfer credits from other institutions, and, of great importance, to learn about financial aid opportunities.

Education Vacations
Eye of the Whale
Foundation for Field Research
Smithsonian Study Tours and Seminars
University Vacations

An educational vacation might be great fun for a change. At Smithsonian Study Tours and Seminars, for example, participants can experience an in-depth exploration of a specific subject or region in the United States or overseas, such as wildlife in India, marine life in Florida, and Civil War sites in Virginia.

Eye of the Whale is an organization that offers an assortment of trips exploring the islands of Kauai, Molokai, and Hawaii, including combinations of whale-watching, trade-wind sailing trips, and hiking across the crater floor of the world's largest active volcano. Nature study, adventure, and relaxation are offered through marine and wilderness experiences.

Many of the folk you'll meet on Foundation for Field Research trips will be living their fantasies of being archaeologists, oceanologists, or primatologists. Past research projects have included: observing chimpanzees in West Africa; digging at archaeological sites in Europe and the Caribbean; and taking a census of whales in the St. Lawrence River, Canada. Volunteers participate under the guidance of professional scientists and researchers. Lengths of stay can vary from two days to one month.

University Vacations offers you gracious living, dining and learning. You can sign up for one- or two-week literature, history, and art programs taught by renowned scholars at fine universities around the world, such as Oxford, Cambridge, Edinburgh, Bologna, Sorbonne, Prague, and Harvard.

(Please see Appendix B for contact information)

Too, let's recognize that the man for you is not necessarily in the places you frequent! What I mean by that is that you, like all of us, have established certain habits and routines - your favorite restaurant, gym, supermarket, house of worship - that you visit regularly. If you are truly serious about finding a fellow, change your routine. Take your morning walk on a different street, have breakfast near the office instead of at home, lunch out of the office instead of in, try a different neighborhood restaurant in another part of town, shop in a different supermarket, join a different gym for three months, log onto a dating site and participate. Be in different places and do different activities so that you'll bump into a new selection of men.

For example, your soul mate could be the owner of a terrific candy store in another part of town whose products you wouldn't touch with a ten foot pole and a place you would never frequent. However, you might just walk by while he's rearranging his windows, and voila! Love at first sight.

It is my sincere belief that you can enrich your life and meet men, too, if you put a bit of time and effort into it. Hopefully, this information I have provided will inspire you to get out and about to create some wonderful adventures for yourself.

Do Something Different!

Explore your interest in participating in new or different activities by answering the following:

1. List your favorite hobbies.

2. Is there a club you can join that revolves around one of them?

3. List your favorite cultural interests.

4. Is there a cultural institution you can visit to meet people with a similar interest?

5. Think of a completely new and different hobby that you would consider trying. When you've chosen it, write it here.

6. Is there a place you'd love to visit but haven't set aside time or money to do so? Where?

7. Can you start planning the trip now? If not, what's the excuse?

8. Will you at least think about planning this trip?

3

TAKE YOUR FACE INTO CYBERSPACE

It's not the men in your life that count; it's the life in your men.
Mae West

One night, I had dinner with some new, single women friends. After one gal learned that I write about the pleasures and dilemmas of over-fifty singlehood, she mentioned that a girlfriend of hers had called her with the name and phone number of a man she met on the Internet.

It was explained that her friend had been browsing the singles' ads online and she spotted an older single guy whose background and credentials looked interesting. Because her friend was married, she encouraged our dinner companion to get in touch with him, as she was from the same town as he.

"A fellow on the Internet?!?" all the other gals exclaimed. "Who would want to do that?"

"I did," answered the gal whose friend was interested in her welfare. "I called him but he didn't sound that interesting. However, I began browsing the Web myself. It's fun, and you never know whom you'll meet."

Subsequently, I kept hearing more and more about it from gals who found the web a fine source for meeting men. In fact, after a few years of talking to Gorgeous Grandmas and further research, I became convinced that the Internet has become the number-one spot to find dates. Consequently, I have partnered with a dating site at my website, *http://www.GorgeousGrandma.com*, which you might like to explore at your leisure.

Perhaps you feel shy about meeting strangers through a computer dating service? I certainly don't blame you. Our generation was taught that men, not us, do the seeking. In fact, when it comes to interacting with strangers (we're not used to that) added to using a device most of us are unfamiliar with (the computer), the whole idea is totally daunting. Add to that our impression that the whole thing is undignified, unladylike, crass, and so forth, and we come up with distaste and a decision not to go there at all.

However, the times and thinking have changed. Most men believe the World Wide Web is a perfectly proper place to meet women. And, many respectable women have changed their thinking to recognize that it's smart to go where the men are.

If you are not computer literate, no problem. Sit next to a friend while she/he does the work for you. Most likely your friends will be delighted to help you improve your social life, and bopping around a dating site can be lots of fun.

Most sites let you browse their members for free. Do so. Choose one of the sites I've suggested and fill in your desired age range for a male and the area code of your city. Their computers do the search for you. After checking out the members in your chosen age range, note the costs and other factors about the site. I would use a notebook for this. After you have visited four or five sites, choose one to explore further.

Some sites are free, until you want to contact the members. Then, there is a cost. Once you visit a few sites, you will easily get the hang of it. You can join conversations in chat rooms, sign up for newsletters, or sign on for a party. There's an assortment of activities at each site. When you touch base with someone, there are a few matters to consider. For one, computer dating can be divided into four phases: online meeting; clicking into private rooms; telephone calls; the real meeting. Don't take too long with your online friendship. Online conversations can move quickly from general topics to intimate ones. Your goal should be to meet the man in person.

Another important issue is safety. Here are some guidelines for internet dating:

* Do not believe everything you read.

* Do not respond to lewd or crude messages.

* Meet in a public place.

* Do not give out your Social Security number, phone number, credit card number, or password.

* Don't reveal too much about your personal life. The medium lends itself to talking about details - personal feelings, family matters, hobbies. By the time you meet him, you may feel you know him, but, of course, you don't.

* Take his phone number if you're interested. When you call, hit *67 from any phone to disable Caller I.D.

* Trust your instincts. If the fellow seems odd, cease all correspondence and change your screen name.

Now, with all this information, where do you find Web sites? On the Internet, of course! I've chosen a few for you as starters:

Gorgeous Grandma Singles Connection (www.GorgeousGrandma.com) I partnered with a fine internet dating site in part because, while running a test, I discovered over 200 men with my area code between the ages of sixty and seventy-five. Those numbers are enticing enough to turn disbelievers into cyber-experts! Membership is free on this site and it includes a number of services. There is a premium membership with additional services which can be paid by the month.

Singles Online (www.singlesonline. com) claims 23,500 members. There is no charge for regular members, but limited access; preferred members pay $9.95 a month, or $59.95 a year, to browse pictures, recorded messages, and extensive biographies. I chose to browse by age (fifty to eighty) and geographic location (all New England states and Florida). I came up with eight men in New England and twenty-five in Florida.

Match.com (www.match.com) is one of the largest online dating services (they tell me) with 100,000 active members. It claims more than 1,200 people have met and married through its service.

Matchmaker (www.matchmaker.com) has a database containing 180,000 profiles. The search is free for two weeks, but after that its per-month charges range from $12.95 to $17.95. A user can browse by location, religion, age, community, lifestyle, and so forth.

Yahoo!Personals (personals.yahoo.com) contains more than 225,000 ads and is free. I chose the age range forty-five to eighty-eight and found 42 men listed in a twenty-five mile range from my postal zip code. For the age range sixty to seventy-eight, twelve listings showed up.

Single Search (www.singlesearch.com) claims 75,000 active members and offers a free ten-day trial. It charges $25 for a one-time search locally to $70 for four worldwide searches.

Jewish Quality Singles (www.jqs.com/main.html) offers profiles divided by sex and decade. Access to profiles is free. To establish contact, it costs $125 for six months and $200 for one year. I found three fellows over sixty - one from New Jersey, one from Canada and one from Delaware. When I lowered the age factor to fifty, there were twenty-seven men.

Confidentially, dear GGs, I am beginning to think that some of our Gorgeous Grandpas fib about their age. I remember when my special person first called me for a blind date, he told me he was fifty-seven. Later, he admitted to sixty-five. Some of the fellows I saw on line noted they were in their sixties but their photographs told me otherwise.

(About disclosing *your* age? I wouldn't. It's rude of a man to ask to begin with and if he is a decent guy, he won't. Men tend to figure it out quickly and once they get to know you, it makes little difference, anyway.)

At any rate, Cybergrandmas, go to it! Have fun, tread softly, and let me know if anything interesting happens. It's a worthwhile adventure and may well be a fruitful one. Stay safe, have a good time, and good hunting!

4

LOOKING GREAT WILL ATTRACT A DATE

Time is a great healer but it's a lousy beautician.
W. Somerset Maugham

Remember the adage "You never get a second chance to make a first impression?" When it concerns what characteristics of a woman appeal to men, certain researchers have discovered that the clothes you wear are secondary to *how well you are groomed.*

In her book, *How to Make Anyone Fall in Love With You,* author Leil Lowndes reveals:

> "... *researchers proved how relatively unimportant a woman's clothes are. Men were shown photographs of women prejudged to be very attractive, moderately attractive, and unattractive. The men expressed interest in having relations with highly attractive and moderately attractive women, no matter how badly they were dressed. No matter how well the unattractive women were dressed, however, overall it was a no-go. Save your expensive clothes to impress your girlfriends or your prospective employer. With men, how you carry yourself, your hair, your nails, your makeup, your grooming, your friendliness - that's what scores.*"

Although I can't agree that men judge a woman's appearance solely by her grooming, I do believe that in order for men to *see* you in the best manner possible, you should put your best *face* forward wherever you go - whether it's to the gym, the supermarket, or walking the dog. Not that a nice face is the only thing that will attract a man, but it sure does help. And, in case you've been letting your appearance slide a bit, let's review some basics so that your *best* face can shine!

Skin, of course, is your first priority, before all the makeup products you use to cover it.

ABOUT SKIN CARE:

My friend, Dotty, asked me to look at a couple of skin-care products she had bought at the doctor's office after her facelift. It seems our plastic surgeons are now offering skin-care products along with in-office representatives to sell them. That would seem to make a lot of sense. Who would know better than our physicians what products are best for proper skin maintenance?

In reality, however, the results these products give often don't justify their high cost. In fact, there are certain products at a Walgreens or CVS (ones dermatologists recommended before they began selling products themselves) that work just as well and for much less money. After all, no product is going to keep one's skin in perfect condition for years, regardless of cost.

Yet, one can't blame our medical gurus for jumping on the skin-care profit wagon. If someone is used to expensive skin-care products, certainly her doctor's wares are a fine way to go, as opposed to Chanel or Sisley, for example, which carry similar price tags.

As a former professional model with the Hart Agency in Boston, I had the opportunity to experiment with a number of beauty products. Many drugstore products were as effective, if not more so, than similar ones found in department stores. Here are some recommendations for products that I have enjoyed:

Night cream: Retin-A. By prescription and the best skin tightener in America. Find a dermatologist for this one, and you won't be sorry. If your skin is sensitive, try Renova first (by prescription also). It's Retin-A combined with a moisturizer. If a good exfoliant/skin-tightener-while-you-sleep is not your cup of tea, try Neutrogena Healthy Skin Anti-Wrinkle Cream or Neutrogena Visibly Firm Night Cream. They contain a more gentle cream than Retin-A and both work well.

Day cream: Any moisturizer in Walgreens! The secret is daily use and changing the brand every six months or so. The effectiveness of the same brand of cream or lotion diminishes with repeated use because the skin becomes used to the ingredients. You'll find a switch to a new product with different ingredients will make a difference. Try a cream rather than a lotion if your skin is dry, because a cream is heavier and will create a thicker film; thus, it will protect the skin longer than a lotion. If you would like a name, try Neutrogena Moisture Lotion, Almay Kinetin Skincare, or Roc Protient Actif Pur Daily Firming Treatment.

Eye cream: Any eye cream in Walgreens or CVS. If it contains a tightening property, all the better. It is best to keep the eye area moisturized all day as well as night. Please don't use face creams around the eyes. Oftentimes, a woman creates bags under her eyes because she's using face cream. The skin around the eyes is very thin, and most creams will make it puffy. L'Oreal Plenitude Line Eraser Eye contains retinol to help reduce crow's feet and wrinkles, but it doesn't sting or irritate the skin.

Cleansing Cream: Cetaphil. It's terrific. You'll find it at Walgreens or Costco. I was a Pond's girl for years until my dermatologist recommended Cetaphil, which works well in combination with the night cream Retin-A because Retin-A has to be applied to a very dry face. If you wash your face with water, you must wait fifteen minutes so that the skin is completely dry before applying Retin-A. Removing makeup with Cetaphil, however, is a time-saver. Cetaphil leaves no residue, and one can use Retin-A immediately thereafter. There's also Neutrogen Deep Clean Cream Cleanser and, for a washcloth-type removal, try Olay Daily Facials.

Exfoliant: Queen Helene Facial Scrub (drugstore), or, if you have sensitive skin, try Clarins. Exfoliating once a week is really important to dislodge dead skin cells. You'll find your face bright and shiny after use.

Moisture Mask: Perfect to use for twenty minutes after exfoliating. Just fine to purchase in the drug store. Try Clarins, if you like department store shopping.

Body Exfoliant: Has your bodice area, between bosoms, become scaly and wrinkled like mother's used to be? Believe it or not, the cause may be nothing more than dead skin! After exfoliating the area, you'll notice a very big difference in suppleness and appearance. Use the Buff Puff (a rough-textured sponge) available at Walgreens. Scrub softly at first. Exfoliating certain areas with a Buff Puff is a "call girl" secret, says the "Mayflower Madam" Sydney Biddle Barrows, who recommends paying attention, also, to the derriere between thighs and buttocks. Then, of course, buff your whole body. An easy once-a-week ritual will pay off in greatly improved skin texture. Another benefit to exfoliation is that afterwards body lotions work one hundred percent better. Because layers of dead skin cells have been whisked away, body cream penetrates with ease.

Body Cream: Anything with aloe in Walgreens. I've used After Tan for years. In addition to softening your skin, it does prolong a tan (and you do use a suntan lotion with an SPF of at least 15, of course). Nivea Body Skin Firming lotion with Q10 is a fine product also.

As a reminder, then, when more of those little wrinkles continue to appear on the skin, a quick and inexpensive skincare program can soften their impact considerably. What's important to remember is: cleansing the skin, exfoliating to get rid of dead skin cells, and moisturizing as a barrier to the elements - a *must-do* program for any woman who cares about her appearance.

Explore these products further by reading labels at a Walmart or a Costco - as well as at Walgreens or CVS. You may be surprised at the similarity of many products' ingredients - but disparity in their price. You don't necessarily have to spend a fortune on department-store enticements and/or products offered by our medical darlings who magically trans-form seventy-year-old faces into fifty-year-old ones.

ABOUT MAKEUP:

Many times over the years, I have been asked my advice on whether women should wear less makeup as they age. My response has been the same each time. How much is not really the issue. Cosmetics are best adapted to the individual and to the characteristics that are unique to you, such as hair color, eye color, skin tone, skin texture, and lifestyle.

Using "less" makeup can mean either using very little makeup or using a number of different cosmetic products within a "natural" color palette. Cosmetics are so very individual that a person can look most attractive within a whole range of looks - from wholesome and little makeup to more makeup and a polished look.

As for minimal makeup, why not? Haven't we all heard the advice that "going natural" is better for an aging face - that certain lipsticks, eye shadows, and blushes are to be avoided because they call attention to a wrinkle or a flaw rather than minimize it?

And, most of us are not in the public eye. We do accept ourselves well at this stage in our lives, I hope, and that means wearing little or no makeup a lot of the time. Are we not loved for our inner qualities rather than for our appearance? Of course. But, right or wrong, like it or not, the world does judge us on how we look most of the time.

It hurts to admit that cosmetics can't provide us with a younger appearance. It would be wonderful to believe in the "cosmetic promise," but no such luck. We all have discovered, to our dismay, that foundation cannot hide poorly maintained skin; eye shadow cannot hide crinkly eyelids; and lipstick cannot hide wrinkled lips. Unfortunately, there seem to be few miracles other than those performed by a surgeon with a scalpel or laser.

The one thing we *can* expect a cosmetic to do is camouflage and soften our surface imperfections. A well-chosen makeup base, for example, matched closely to our skin color can soften and tone down our facial wrinkles. Mascara on our lashes can enhance the lovely color of our eyes. Eyeliner on the upper lids of our eyes can subtly define the eye, particularly for the blonder GG.

Eye shadow can be a choice, even for those of us with crinkly lids. Keeping it to a soft, neutral matte color (nude or peach) is wise, though. Blush is very helpful for a sallow or pale complexion. A soft peach or rose color will do, applied with a light hand and a soft blush brush. Lip liner is a wonderful tool for combating wrinkles around the lips. Too, many of us have suffered from "bleeding" lipstick. A liner color closely matched to a lipstick color keeps our lip color in balance as well as helps our lipstick stay in place. The fashion of dark lipstick today does not work for us GGs - unless the facelift is new and you really are gorgeous. If so, go to it.

It's difficult to recommend specific colors in makeup because each of us has different skin tones and tastes. Yet, you might appreciate knowing about a few cosmetic lines in order to ease the confusion when there are so many brands to choose from. I'm pleased to recommend those products that have worked for me through the years, along with some new ones I've discovered as well:

FACE:

Foundation: Ultra-super important to use to protect your skin from the elements but not necessary to wear when you're at the gym. For light coverage, I prefer a tinted moisturizer by Nivea, Lancome, or Clarins. In the evening for more coverage, try Prescriptives or L'Oreal. Chanel and Sisley are good, too, but pricey. A word of warning: be very careful that your foundation is the right color to blend with your neck. Otherwise, you may well have a very noticeable difference in color between them.

Concealer: M.A.C. Cosmetics has a nice one. So does Maybelline Cover Stick, Clinique Quick Protector, and Trish McEvoy. Most beauty experts will recommend that your concealer be a little lighter than your skin tone. A few cosmetic lines offer concealers with two different products for coverage. Yellow is for camouflaging dark circles.

Powder: If you want your foundation to stay on all day, powder is the answer. However, be very light-handed with it. In fact, if you use a powder puff for application, be sure to use a soft brush to smooth it. Oftentimes, too much powder will exaggerate wrinkles, not diminish them. As for a brand, probably the one you are using is fine. Just be sure the powder is not too heavy. Typically, the cosmetic lines that favor makeup artists and models carry a powder that's used for the fashion runway. It can be too heavy-duty and is really best for younger skin.

Blush: It's a very nice product for most of us over fifty since the blush of youth has dimmed a bit. Just be careful to not apply it on the apple of your cheek as it can look fake. I like to use a bronzer color for its more natural-looking qualities rather than a pink or rose color. However, a cosmetician can easily help you with a color choice so as to acquire a natural look. I have found Guerlain to have the best choice of color in a bronzer. For a Walgreens buy, try L'Oreal Feel Naturale Light Softening Blush.

EYES:

Eyebrows: Well-shaped brows are key to a youthful appearance. Put the pencil aside and use an angled brush with a powder. Use powder one shade lighter than your natural color because it darkens as you wear it.

Eyeshadow sold in drugstores and discount stores is just as good as those found in department store lines. The color selections are extensive and wouldn't you prefer spending just a few dollars rather than over ten dollars? What I do recommend, however, is every six months or a year, have your face made up by a department store makeup artist to keep you contemporary with current makeup colors and application. If you haven't already done so, consider learning to use makeup brushes, particularly for your eyes, rather than the dabbers that come packaged in eyeshadow boxes. There's a world of difference in the subtleties a person can perform with a brush as opposed to a teeny plastic stick with a cotton ball top.

Mascara is very personal. I assume by now that you have found a particular mascara that works well for your lashes. For years, I was using Lancome thickener because my lashes were very fine and almost nil. Lately, however, I found that Max Factor 2000 and L'Oreal Voluminous were just as good for one-third the price. And black has always been my chosen color. Many gals like Maybelline Great Lash Mascara, also.

Eyeliner is again a personal choice. I have very small eyes and, without a definition of some sort, my eyes just recede into my face. I used to use a soft pencil in brown or green. Again, lately, I have found a liquid liner pen by M.A.C. that works just great. It comes in both black and brown, and it's very easy to use. I do warn against using black liner, though. It can be terribly harsh, particularly on older faces. Brighten your eyes with white eye pencil just above the lashes of your lower lids.

LIPS:

Lipstick: Again, color is personal choice. However, I believe we over fifty can look rather sallow and colorless in the brown-toned lipsticks that have been so popular these last few years. Be really careful in your color choice. And, I have found the drugstore to have an excellent color selection in a variety of lines.

Lipliner: I think the lipliner is the greatest invention for us over fifty since underwire bras. What does occur is that our top lip narrows as we age. With a lipliner, we can easily camouflage that process. Too, a lipliner can be applied over the entire lip to help lipstick stay on longer. Try it. As for color, I recommend keeping the lipliner as close to your lipstick color as possible. Also, using a lipbrush can lengthen the staying power of lipstick on your lips as well as increase the life of the lipstick.

HAIR:

Color: Your hairdresser is the best judge of style and haircolor. What I believe is important to emphasize here is that if your quest is for a man at this time in your life, get rid of the gray. I know that some of you like it and maybe the children do too; however, men are intensely sight-oriented creatures and, if the rest of you comes across as youthful, shouldn't you give that same message with your hair-color? If your hair is naturally dark, try lightening it just a little to a cognac or tortoiseshell brown. A comfortable way to determine your best look and color might be to visit a wig store and try on a few.

Length: Research has proven that men like long, straight hair. Longer tresses can look great if the cut is soft and well done. However, as we grow older, the longer our hair is below our chin line, the more length we add to our faces. When a woman's hair is too long, her lines and wrinkles become more prominent.

Do be careful not to overdo makeup. As some of us age, we can lose perspective and, unfortunately, apply too much. There are men out there who are turned off by women who are overly concerned about their appearance.

One man's observation:

I went out with a woman once who cared so much about how she looked in bed that I got totally turned off. First of all, she came to bed perfectly made up, lipstick and all, and with loads of jewelry on — about four gold chains, bracelets, rings on half her fingers. She had these really long nails, the kind that look like claws, and she would touch me carefully so that she wouldn't break her nails. The whole time we were having sex, she kept arranging herself so that she looked good, stopping to run her fingers through her hair, or straighten her necklaces. I couldn't wait to get out of there.

ABOUT COSMETIC SURGERY:

One evening at a glamorous cocktail party, Sally was delighted to see Jane, a former neighbor. As they were chatting, Sally mentioned her recent divorce and her thoughts about making a change to her lifestyle. Jane's first comment to Sally was: "Why don't you think about sprucing up your appearance a bit first?" When Sally complained that her income was not what it used to be and her disposable income was strictly limited, Jane commented: "I'd rather spend my money on my face than on these," pointing to the pretty diamonds dangling from a chain around Sally's neck.

If you are thinking about a little nip and tuck, perhaps I'm not the first to encourage you to do it. It doesn't change your appearance (unless you have your chin line changed, or such) as much as it makes you look refreshed and less wrinkled. It's a great corrector of flaws.

Some gals won't even consider surgery because they think anyone who does it is overly vain. But, I think you are entitled to look as good as you can. Now that the kids are grown and that stage of life has passed, you can spend a bit of your hard-earned money on yourself. And, as a single woman in search of love, you want to pretty yourself for the romance that will, most assuredly, be entering your life.

If you are reluctant to undergo surgery, botox and collagen treatments offered by dermatologists are quite nice. Also, laser is something to consider. I do recommend avoiding people called aestheticians who offer these services, though, unless they are board-certified to perform them. There are too many newcomers to this field who have little experience. Seek out plastic surgeons or dermatologists instead.

ABOUT WEIGHT:

Are you comfortable at the weight you are? Or do you honestly feel that a weight-loss program would be in your best interest? When it comes to meeting a fellow, do you accept the fact that being overweight might decrease your chances for a date?

To be perfectly blunt, in order to catch a man's eye, a woman needs to be not only well groomed but also on the slender side.

I know, I know. Most of us are tired of thinking about pounds and how to take them off. If I can encourage but one change in your life, however, it is a good weight-loss and exercise program. It may well be the most effective boost to your health and self-esteem you can make to date.

My quest for a smaller waistline has been ongoing for years. I've kept myself posted on the newest in diet pills, educated myself with each new diet book, and I've starved myself beyond belief. I succeed in losing weight from time to time, but inevitably the waistline expands once more. Also, my special person often orders dessert, which leaves me the sickening choice of whether or not to try some.

I know I'm not alone in this struggle. Unless you are skinny by nature, you, too, have put on pounds over the years. Research has proven that most women gain on average 2.5 pounds a year after the age of thirty-five. It's simply our genetics . . . and it's lousy.

What can we do about it?

It's simple. Just diet. And I have a few to recommend to you:

The Cabbage Soup Diet, for one. I weighed myself on the *second day* of this diet and saw that I had lost one and a half pounds!! To see my weight loss so quickly motivated me to keep going. That's what I'd been missing all the while on those other diets. This visible jump-start was the indicator that my body recognized my desire to lose weight, and it was talking back to me. I stayed on that diet for three weeks and lost about twelve pounds.

It's cabbage soup, fruit and vegetables for the first three days. Then it changes to other foods, which makes the diet more interesting. Variations on this diet were conceived by Susan Estrich, a lawyer with a keen sense of humor, whose book is a lot of fun to read. The name of the book is *Making the Case for Yourself: A Diet Book for Smart Women*. There are many other cabbage soup diets around, and, from what I've heard, they all work.

Another diet I recently attempted and like better than Cabbage Soup is one that required assistance from a hypnotist. I was amazed that my visit to him for one hour every other week could result in my losing thirty pounds! It took me eight months. The session consists of his hypnotizing me *not* to eat more than 1,000 calories a day, *not* to eat more than one-half the food on my plate, and to drink lots of water between meals. He provided me with a comprehensive book on calorie content while instructing me to write down the calorie count of each meal.

My girlfriend has had unusual success with Overeaters Anonymous. She lost 40 pounds and continues to lose a pound a month. There are weekly meetings in practically every city around the country. Check their website for information: http//www.OvereatersAnonymous.org.

Even though a woman's overall appearance is important, we know also that the right chemistry between a woman and a man is the other vital ingredient to attraction. Although many men confess a preference for a certain physical type or for a particular hair color or body shape, most fellows are not foolish enough to rule out women who do not fit into their narrow category. It merely takes the right woman who ignites the right chemistry between them to change a man's impression.

To ignite that chemistry, here are some recommendations for making that top-notch first impression:

1. **Always be well-groomed.** A nice appearance includes: no poorly fitting or completely outdated clothes; no run-down heels, chipped nails, or

unkempt hair; no bra straps showing or runs in pantyhose; no chipped nail polish. Men are visual creatures, and their reactions are immediate.

2. **Look feminine**. Dress tastefully to look soft, alluring, and approachable. Stay away from business attire as dating attire. If you're wearing a suit (which announces "unapproachable"), leave the jacket unbuttoned.

3. **Maintain a regular weekly exercise program.** Not only is a program top-notch for maintaining health and losing weight, but the gym is a great place to meet men.

4. **Don't wear too much jewelry.** The rule of five is a good standard to follow. For example: one pair of earrings (counts as 1); a watch (2); a ring (3); a pin or necklace (4); perhaps a bracelet (5). More than that and the look screams "flashy." **Important note:** do not wear rings on your left hand. Men often mistake a decorative ring for a marriage band.

5. **Don't wear ultra-long nails.** The message here is that you're self-indulgent, frivolous, and inconsiderate. Men don't understand the look, the expense, and how they can be in bed with you without getting hurt.

6. **Don't groom yourself in public (comb hair, use lipstick/lipliner at the table).** I know that you don't comb your hair in public because you're too much of a lady to do so. However, I do know that most of us are in the habit of putting lipstick on at a restaurant table because it was a perfectly acceptable act when we were married. However, now that you are single, don't do it. It's a habit most men don't like.

7. **Don't use strong perfume.** Most men really object to it. Be sure to check with a friend and her opinion on your favorite fragrance, particularly before a first date. If you live in a warm climate, a perfume's essence becomes even stronger when the weather is warm and humid.

8. **Don't use heavy makeup, dark lipstick, black eyeliner.** A total turnoff to men is too much makeup. Although dark lipstick is the vogue for our younger sisters, be very careful with it. It can be deadly for wrinkled skin, small lips, and very white complexions. Black eyeliner is always a no-no. It's too intense for a pretty look, and it can make one's eyes look smaller.

There is no such thing as an ugly woman, only a lazy one.
- Helena Rubinstein

5

BE ADAPTABLE AND RISK NEW ADVENTURES

If you are bent on succeeding, you must be a risk-taker. Don't be afraid to go out on a limb because that is where the fruit is.

Have you ever been in the company of a friend who was so narrow-minded and unbending that you wanted to shake her? How about being around someone who refused to understand the meaning of the word compromise? Or, even more maddening, your single buddies (or perhaps you, too) have grown stubbornly inflexible when it comes to trying new activities, adventures, sports, or travel spots, or to dating a different type of man than they've ever experienced?

I know that we all get into a rut as we age, regardless of marital status, and we do develop fears that are for the most part, unfounded. Unfortunately, the result is that, out of habit, we seek approval from trusted folk around us, even when it comes to moving about in the dating world. Don't you find that the older some women get, the more judgmental about the smallest matters they become?

My job, however, is not to comment on the foibles and attitudes of women as they age; my sincere desire is to motivate you to become adaptable, flexible, understanding, and less judgmental. Plus, my intent is to encourage you to make your own decisions on dating matters and not follow a rigid set of rules. Oftentimes, our well-intentioned married friends advise us on dating from mere observation, not from first-hand experience (unless they're not telling all!).

One of my girlfriends told me about her friend, Marcia, who was having "the time of her life" seeing a guy she met at a hotel pool in Florida - a cabana boy. Marcia is in her sixties, divorced, good-looking, financially secure, and apparently adventurous. This fellow is an "early Marlon Brando type - in his thirties," exclaims my girlfriend, "and you should see his pecs!"

I'm not sharing this story with you to either recommend or condemn Marcia's choice (far be it for this GG to be so judgmental). I am discussing this little adventure with you to mention that, at first, Marcia was embarrassed to be seen with her "Marlon." She asked my friend what she should do. My friend recommended to Marcia that she should absolutely, positively "have a ball!"

To suggest that he might be a gigolo is too obvious. (Hopefully, Marcia was savvy enough to take those all-too-important precautions during sex.) What I want to emphasize here is that a smart fellow-GG gave her approval to a friend to do something that our generation would not have thought was acceptable behavior a few years ago.

Herein lies a fine example of how our social norms, our standards for appropriate dating behavior have changed. "Marlon" is half Marcia's age and has a moderate income. But what difference does it make to Marcia? She's happy, he's happy, and her friend gave her blessing, which makes the two friends happy. (We do like to have approval from our friends, sometimes).

More about being adaptable - perhaps you have been thinking about placing a personal ad. Thanks to those dramatically shifting social standards, as we discussed in chapter 3, personal ads are now quite acceptable. In fact, remember that most men believe that ads are one of the most favorable ways to meet women.

Advertising for relationships became popular in the late eighties. However, most proper, respectable, mature single women felt it was demeaning and undignified, and they did not begin to participate until the early nineties. By that time, those more adventurous GGs had discovered that not only were their daughters answering and placing ads, but that they were meeting and marrying some very nice young men.

Take my friend, Sandi, a widow who has been alone for about seven years. Once over her bereavement, she began to go out a lot - with the girls. After a few years, she and I talked about how to bring some men into her life. When I suggested she try the personals, she would not hear of it. "Absolutely not," she said. "I couldn't possibly meet a stranger, in a strange place, without knowing anything about him. Plus, what if he doesn't like me? I hate rejection!"

"Really, Sandi," I said. "There's no one I know who likes to be rejected. But if you don't risk, you don't gain."

During the following year, Sandi told me numerous stories of married friends who promised to fix her up and never did. It seemed the longer Sandi waited for someone to fix her up, the more lonely and frustrated she became.

Sandi is typical of so many single women who believe that friends will help them to meet new people and to have an active social life. Unfortunately, it's not so. This is not to say that some friends don't try. But married folk generally know few singles. One's best chance for meeting new faces is to step outside the small, narrow, familiar world of married couples and enter a much larger universe.

Not only are there fewer men out there for us maturing, wise, and sexy creatures, but we have gained the wisdom to be choosy about the types of men we wish to be associated with. To be perfectly blunt, the only way you can meet your prince is to have a great many frogs to choose from. After all, the more particular you are, the less compatible you become with the majority (which we'll talk about in the next chapter).

Finally, Sandi's friend, Roberta, became so dismayed at Sandi's negative attitude that Roberta wrote and placed a personal for Sandi. Sandi sounded very happy about it. So was I. Did she meet anyone through the first ad? No. She received not one response. But I was proud of her. She kept a stiff upper lip, bounced back from the disappointment, ran the ad again, and received four responses the second time. She had coffee with two of the men she heard from and found them pleasant but no cigar. The third man turned out to be a fellow she knew from high school, and the fourth one had no interest in her after the initial introduction. With more confidence, she placed another ad, in a different paper, and received six responses. She started to date a fellow from her third ad attempt, and he was quite a charmer.

Yes, a lot of gals are changing their thinking. As independent, smart, wise, single women, they recognize that their male counterparts out there are diminishing each year. Did you know that there are eighty-three men for every one hundred women between the ages of sixty-five and sixty-nine? Did you know that the proportion of men is reduced by half after age eighty-five, where there are only forty-two men for every one hundred women?

The time has come to put to rest your safe, habitual, outdated ideas! If you are to change, grow, relish, and embrace your present life and enrich, enhance, and reinvent your future years, it is in your best interest to open your eyes, your mind, and your heart, to take in some different experiences.

I used to be a very conservative person, and I still am in a number of ways. Yet, I discovered early on, as I started to socialize after divorce, that if I couldn't or wouldn't change the situation I was in, I had to change my thinking about that situation. Hence, in order for me to feel comfortable mingling with strangers and in more diverse social groups than I had been accustomed to in the past, I had to become more flexible, less judgmental, kinder to myself when I made a blunder, more courageous when I ventured out to meet new people, and more assertive in taking risks than I had been in my married state. And I had to shorten that list - that very long list - of criteria a man had to meet. Fortunately, I finally got smarter, the list became shorter (we'll talk about your list later), and a special person came into my life.

∽∾

A single life can be full of nice surprises, though. In spite of all we endured on our bumpy road toward singlehood, a great many of us discovered a new type of freedom, independence, and, to our relief, renewed confidence.

> *Dear GG:*
>
> *I was a homemaker for twenty-five years. I only knew how to cook a meal and change a diaper. I had no self-esteem, no notion that I might have a few brains of my own, and no money that I could spend without my husband's approval.*
>
> *My husband paid all the bills. I couldn't balance a checkbook and knew nothing about car payments, mortgages, health insurance or interest rates.*
>
> *Divorce changed all that. I am now remarried, run my own business, balance four checkbooks, do payroll and all the bookkeeping. I deal with business accounts, workers' compensation, liability insurance and unemployment.*
>
> *I learned the hard way that I could make it on my own if I had to and I am very proud of myself.*
>
> *Frances G., Mashpee, MA*

Where does that confidence come from? It comes from being willing to take risks; being willing to face rejection and move on; and believing in the value of ourselves. Oftentimes, though, our sensitive feelings can be a big deterrent for those of us who are alone, while we attempt bravely to reestablish and to nurture that delicate confidence and self-esteem.

As a result, fear about being rejected has caused many of us to avoid the unknown, postpone taking a risk, or put off taking that step into new, untested waters. But, one manner of addressing that dilemma is to bumble ahead enthusiastically and to deal with it as it happens, if it happens. Usually, the worst that can happen is not so bad after all.

I have a tale.

As research for my column and the fifty-and-over singles series, my editor assigned me to visit a disco club located on Boston's north shore - alone. Yes, alone. It took a little while to work up the courage to face that new and different world unescorted. But I did, and I went.

The parking lot was totally empty when I drove up, and I thought the place was closed. Nope. It was just 8:30 p.m., and I was a bit early, said the greeter, who then requested my two-dollar cover charge. After 10:00 p.m., he explained, the cover goes to five dollars. Most of the people will arrive just before the price change, he said.

So they did, and the place began to fill up by 9:45. Meanwhile, I had been enjoying a long chat with a nice lady bartender who explained that the people they usually drew on Tuesdays were between the ages of forty and seventy; that many of them were regulars; that the group mix is not only singles but also married couples who like to dance; that in the wintertime they draw about two hundred to three hundred people; that in the summertime the crowd grows considerably.

I noticed a gentleman sitting a few seats away, and after I completed an exploratory walk around the place, Peter ("believe it or not, my last name is Smith") and I started to chat. He was a tall, charming, well-spoken, good-looking guy, not married (he said), a builder, a golfer, a member of a country club, had a home in Florida, and so forth. We discovered quickly that we had a number of interests in common. After a while, I put away my working gear (pen, paper, glasses), relaxed, and began to enjoy his company and the music.

Long story short: Peter and I talked and danced the night away. When I recognized that the evening was growing late and that I had an hour's drive ahead of me, I mentioned to Peter I was leaving and asked the bartender for my bill. Peter immediately offered to pay my check and to take me out for coffee before my long ride home, but first "Excuse me a second while I go to the men's room. I'll be right back."

After waiting ten minutes, I became restless. I walked out to the entryway and asked a man coming out of the men's room if there was a fellow there who was not feeling well, perhaps. "No," he said, "there's no one in there."

Aw. C'mon. Peter's joking with me. He'll show up any second.

Well, he didn't.

Why did he disappear? I have absolutely no idea. We were having a fine time. The bill was small, and I don't think that really entered into it. And he gave me a very strong impression that we would be seeing one another again, even though we had not exchanged phone numbers.

Is this type of incident something we singles should adapt to when we socialize out there? I don't know. I really don't know. I have concluded, though, that what we might try to be is intelligent about this kind of thing. Perhaps we should consider what our expectations are about a meeting of this sort, although I don't think I expected anything.

Hold it. Sure I did. I expected this person to return from the men's room. I believed this man when he said he would be right back. I did not have any reason to believe he would not.

He lied about coming back. Thus, I assume he lied about a lot of the other things we talked about. Wonderful. What a waste of an evening.

Was it really wasted? On second thought, not really. I made some useful observations about singles gatherings, as well as, alas, picking up a lesson in living.

Did I learn anything else? Well, I must admit it was great fun to talk with Peter, dance with him, and listen to music.

On the other hand, there were other fellows asking me to dance, to whom I said yes on occasion, but I spent the majority of my time there with Peter. Perhaps I should not have. Perhaps I should have been wiser and socialized in a different manner. Maybe I have learned a lesson. Maybe, the next time I find myself in similar circumstances (if I do), I will do things differently.

Even though feeling rejected is tough, I have enough self-respect, confidence, and experience, fortunately, to recognize that I was none the worse for wear.

What can we conclude? Perhaps, when we do feel rejected, it would be helpful to catch our breath, pause, and think about it - rationally and unemotionally - rather than blame ourselves for not being nice enough, pretty enough, smart enough, something enough.

Perhaps, most of the time, it's not us. Perhaps, more often, it is the shortcomings and inadequacies in the other person that bring about such rude and thoughtless behavior.

Perhaps, fate might have it that one night I shall return, and I will see that Peter-person face-to-face. When I do - rationally and without emotion, of course - Pow! Right in the kisser!

The same girlfriend who shared the "Marlon" story soon touched me with another story. It seems a neighbor came to her not too long ago complaining of terrible black-and-blue marks all over her body. When she visited the doctor that same day, she was told she had an advanced case of leukemia and that she had less than a month to live. No warning signs, no pain, no nothing. And, yes, she died - very fast.

Please do not misunderstand when I suggest taking a risk. I do not recommend total recklessness in your life, carefree abandon in your thinking, thoughtless chaos in your dating, or a rest-of-the-world-be-damned attitude. What I am suggesting is that you make an effort to thrive, not merely survive.

Savor and participate in life today. You owe it to yourself to make your life, single or not, a rich and rewarding one.

Some suggestions to think about:

Be adaptable. If you find yourself opinionated, narrow in thought, never willing to be led rather than lead, perhaps dating should not yet be on your agenda. In order to get along with the different types of men you are going to meet, it's in your best interest to be adaptable and easy to get along with. Remember, dating is supposed to be fun!

Take a risk by doing something different. It is important that you make your own experiences in life rather than sit back expecting a social life to come to you. It will not happen. Your success in finding your one and only depends solely on how hard you want to work to find him. You and only you create your own destiny. If you have never been to a stock-car race, try it for the fun of it. If you have never been to a carnival, go to one. Do something every so often to bring a new experience into your life. And try participating by yourself. It's comfortable attending events with a friend, but it can be an adventure to go alone. You never know whom you might meet.

Don't be judgmental. It is in your best interest to have few expectations when you start dating again. Men are wary of women who jump to conclusions early, and they flee from gals who want to extract promises after the second or third date. Being open and nonjudgmental will allow you to enjoy the lovely surprises that may very well happen along the way. For instance, not being judgmental will allow a less-than-perfect man to enter your life who may, given time, end up as your Mr. Perfect.

Be open to the less-than-perfect man. It takes time to to learn a man's best qualities. If you insist on dating only great-looking or exciting or intriguing or wealthy men, you are severely limiting your selection. There aren't that many choices at this stage in our lives. It's better to be open and amenable to a wide range of personalities and incomes.

Don't think about rejection. Surely, none of us likes to be rejected. It's embarrassing and a terrible slap to the ego. However, it is a fact of life that it does happen every so often, particularly in the dating world. Don't let it get to you! Learn to put those slights aside and move on - fast! Believe Eleanor Roosevelt when she said, "Nobody can make you feel inferior without your permission."

Don't give up on men. In your quest for a life's companion, it is very hard to keep putting yourself out there if you have had repeatedly disappointing or unfulfilling relationships. I want to encourage you, however, to keep trying. Giving up will not enhance your life, it will depress you and lead to feelings of bitterness. You don't want that to happen, and I certainly don't want that to happen to you. There is a man out there for you. Get going, girl! He's waiting for you to find him.

From Erica Jong in *Fear of Fifty* (Random House):

"Some women I know have given up on men because they cannot stand the pain. What pain? The pain of seeing 50-year old men going out with 28-year old 'step-daughters.' The pain of waiting for telephone calls that never come, the pain of needing too much, wanting too much, and so deciding, once and for all, to stop wanting men. You can train

yourself to do this. You can be like the man who trains his horse to need less and less food, and who is astonished when at last the horse dies. You can seal off your skin, your eyes, your mouth. But sooner or later love will come claim you. You will dry up like a brittle flower and a breath of wind will blow your pale powder away. I would rather stay open to love even though love means disorder, possibly pain. How many times have I redone the curtains and bookshelves? How many times have I undone my life? I hate the chaos, but it has also kept me young."

DATING ATTITUDE QUIZ*

It's important to be adaptable when you date. But, do you have a positive attitude about dating? Or have you had a few unpleasant or difficult experiences that have turned you off?

Answer the following questions to explore how positive or negative your attitude really is. Choose **one** answer to each question you believe expresses your true feelings, and circle the letter of your choice.

1. My belief about men is that "they" . . .

    a. Simply cannot be trusted.

    b. Are basically decent, but none of them really interests me.

    c. Are mostly a bunch of losers, users, and jerks.

    d. Include many interesting, charming, sexy potential friends and lovers.

    e. Will be mostly incompatible with me because I have only one perfect soulmate.

2. Dating is . . .

    a. A necessary and useful social tool for creating and making personal choices.

    b. A futile exercise in ego degradation.

    c. A chance to meet new men who could be a lot of fun.

    d. A chance to have sex with no commitments.

    e. Something only younger folks do.

*adapted from Datesmart Quiz by Dana Peach at http://www. thirdage.com

3. The most important aspect of a date is . . .

a. How I look.

b. How much money my date spends on me.

c. Whether I enjoy myself enough to repeat the experience.

d. Where we go.

e. Whether or not I have great sex.

4. When I meet someone new . . .

a. I have a series of important questions I ask him immediately to not waste time on losers.

b. I know whether I will like him in one second.

c. I've given up on meeting new men because they never are my type.

d. I look forward to the new experiences they may introduce into my life.

e. Before considering him marriage material, I want to know a man a bit.

5. Successful dating . . .

a. Is a horrible game only the rich, beautiful, and manipulative can win.

b. Involves a set of basic skills most people can learn and benefit from.

Circle below your answer to each question. Write the number assigned to your answer on the right. Total the Column to find your score.

Question #1: (a) -5; (b) 0;(c) -5; (d) 10; (e) 0 _____ *10.*

Question #2: (a) 10; (b) -5; (c) 5; (d) 0; (e) 0 _____ *5*

Question #3: (a) 0; (b) 0; (c) 10; (d) 0; (e) 0 _____ *10*

Question #4: (a) -5; (b) 0; (c) -5; (d) 10; (e) 5 _____ *10*

Question #5: (a) -5; (b) 10 _____ *10*

Total score _____ *45*

If your score is between -20 and 19 - Oops. Better reconsider your beliefs. If you are still sitting back and not participating in the single life, jump in and start dating!

Between 20 and 39 - It may take some luck for you to find a truly compatible partner. You'll probably get by but you won't have nearly as much fun as you could be having.

Between 40 and 50 - Congratulations! You will have lots of pleasurable dating moments ahead of you and, most likely, one of those dates will be with the partner of your dreams.

OBSERVATIONS:

Regarding Question #1: Negating strangers before we meet them serves no purpose and makes it impossible to meet someone new. Total distrust of men is an attitude that's hard to hide. By narrowing your choice to "one perfect soulmate," you have reduced your chances considerably. The attitude a smart woman has is an adaptable one. Men are basically decent and there are any number of possibilities for a romantic relationship.

Regarding Question #2: Only among the more mature women and men has dating had a chance to evolve. Dating at this stage in our lives is between people who recognize their individuality, desires, values, and goals on a far greater scale than they did in their younger years.

Regarding Questions #3: What matters on a date is the pleasure of a man's company. The only thing the smart woman decides at the end of the date is whether or not she wants to see the man again. Your dating life will improve immeasurably if you keep in mind that the first goal of dating is to have some fun. The smart woman saves serious expectations only for a person she knows very, very well.

Regarding Question #4: Men do not come in "types"; they are very individualistic. Many men dislike the dating experience because they are given the third degree. When a woman makes a quick judgement on a man, she may often lose out on a winner. A healthy dating attitude consists of having a firm grip on fundamental values while opening yourself to new adventures.

Regarding Question #5: Dating is based on the the same fundamental skills as marriage: honesty, openness, compassion, the ability to listen, a taste for simple pleasures. These skills can be acquired and learned although, dear GGs, I sense that most of you have already acquired them.

- college educ. ~~of~~
- earns at least 50,000
- not overweight
- fun /stim to be w
- compassionate/
  empathetic/
  listener
- likes to touch
- good lover
- can relate to
  my kids

Get Real About the Man You Want

You can't have everything. Where would you put it?
Steve Wright

Now that we've talked about how dating differs at this age, where to find men, refreshing one's appearance, and how adapting well brings choices, let's move on to explore the importance of being realistic.

Denise writes:

"I had a wonderful forty-three-year love affair with my wonderful husband and then he passed away. I have four great children, eight grandchildren, lots of friends, and activities galore. Yet, there was nothing satisfying me until I began to date an old school chum who was a widower. We fell in love (both in our sixties) and life again became very special. A few months ago he, too, passed away, and once again I find myself longing for male companionship. The desire is so strong that I feel like half a person."

Denise speaks for millions of women who are unhappy without male companionship. But, the quest for love and romance is so much easier if a woman can identify: *why* she looks for love; the type of man she *needs, not wants,* and; the importance of *being realistic, not idealistic*, in her goals.

STEP ONE:

Why do women look for love? For most, it is a combination of factors:

* to enhance life by sharing it with another person;
* for intimacy, a sharing of feelings;
* for sexual pleasure;
* for a man's friendship and companionship;
* for social maneuverability.

Most women agree there is a feeling a woman gets by loving a man that one cannot get anywhere else. "I don't know if I miss sex," Janet, a widow friend, says. "But I miss my husband's arm around me and the way he cradled me when I slept."

And then there are women who look for companionship for other reasons:

※ To improve their financial security;

※ To stop feeling lonely;

※ To improve a low self-esteem because of the lack of a relationship;

※ To make a former partner jealous;

※ To improve their social life in a couples' world;

※ To heal the hurt from a former relationship.

When a woman looks for love with these criteria in mind, she could be headed for trouble. When finances are involved, for example, a woman would expect her partner to have a high degree of financial security. Should he suffer a sudden financial reversal, the future of that relationship is questionable. Regarding the other criteria, she is hurting psychologically. A woman should heal her anxieties regarding a former relationship, lack of one, or her social needs, before she enters into a new relationship.

Oftentimes, underlying sociological factors take over in a search for a mate. More than likely, the man you seek will share your attitudes and values. Research has proven that most couples are from similar backgrounds. The wealthy marry the wealthy, lower-income men marry lower-income women, and so on.

And, probably the man you will be attracted to will have a personality very different from yours. Research tells us that the confident marry the insecure, the meek marry the quick-tempered, and so forth. Generally, people seek mates who complement them and offer qualities they lack.

One rather bizarre example of romantic preference are the professional women who find male prisoners appealing. When I mentioned this fact during a speaking engagement one night, a gal in the audience corrected me to say that it is not merely convicts that interest certain women, it is convicted murderers, as well. In the *New York Times Magazine* article, "Men, Women, Sex, and Darwin," the anthropologist Sarah Blaffer Hardy observes:

> "... *when female status and access to resources do not depend on their mates' status, women will likely use a range of criteria not primarily or even necessarily prestige or wealth, for mate selection. (There is a) 1996 New York Times story about women from a wide range of professions - bankers, judges, teachers, journalists - who marry male convicts. The allure of such a man is not their income, for you can't earn much when you make license plates for a living. Instead, it's the men's gratitude that proves irresistible. The women also like the fact that their husbands' fidelity is guaranteed."*

Some women choose to marry younger men. I can count at least six women I know who pride themselves on bragging about how many years older they are than their husbands. There are from five to ten years separating the ages of the husbands from the wives, and they all have been happily married for a good length of time. I do, however, have a tale about a sixty-year-old woman who married a thirty-something fellow that is not a happy one. I hope it's not typical of an older woman marrying a younger man, but being forewarned is being forearmed.

It seems a gal living in California complained to friends for years how lonely she was. Finally, on her return from a month's trip to Europe, she landed with lots of goodies, including a boy-toy in tow who could not speak English. After endowing him with clothes, jewelry, a car, language lessons, and full run of her house for six months, they were married.

Two years later, this boy-toy was seen cuddling one night in the corner of a lovely cafe with a sweet, young thing who was obviously not his wife. A few weeks later, he was spotted again, at another restaurant, being cutesy with another lovely, also not his wife. It seems she was out of town.

Did he live happily ever after as a well-cared-for husband/gigolo? No way. He came home one day from his tennis game to find his clothes on the front lawn and the marriage over.

Another woman who lived and supported a younger man for several years had this to say:

> *"What finally brought me to my senses was the way he looked at me one day when I mentioned that I was ten years old when World War II ended. But, that only was the tip of the iceberg. He used drugs. I drank martinis. My idea of a great night out was to go to the theater, his was to go roller skating. I decided I did not want to share the rest of my life or even another month with a man who shared so few memories and values with me - no matter how good he was in bed."*

Why *do you* look for love? It might be helpful for you to write a personal essay to yourself about it. Please take your time and be truly honest.

After you have thought deeply about why you desire love, let us move on to explore together how to find the type of man you need.

STEP TWO:

It is important to recognize that, as a mature and experienced woman, you *must know yourself* and *respect the person you are* before you are able to judge what type of man would be good for you. Once you have assessed those attributes, you will be able to narrow down wisely the qualities that you would like a man to have. But let's not make them too narrow. My self-appointed mission is to encourage you to broaden, not minimize, your vision and your opportunities,

Begin by asking yourself:

※ Are you interested in a relationship that has it all - sex, friendship, romance, intimacy, passion, love, - or just some?

※ Do you wish to remarry or do you want companionship and intimacy just part-time?

※ Do you expect your special someone to fit into your lifestyle or are you adaptable enough to adjust to whatever occurs?

※ Are you so terribly lonely that anyone will fill the bill; or

※ Are you fussy, fussy, fussy?

To help you assess your needs further, you will also want to consider:

※ His physical characteristics, if that is major to you. Remember, however, that lasting relationships consist of shared interests, mutual respect, and devotion to one another - not a handsome face or the right height or weight.

※ His ability to make you feel secure.

※ His money, power, and accomplishments, if those factors are important to you.

※ His religious affiliation, if that is important to you.

※ His need or desire for a permanent relationship.

❋ His interests, lifestyles, values, goals.

❋ His ability satisfy your needs.

Another consideration is the extent of your flexibility. Here are some questions to help you determine your flexibility about choosing a partner. Circle T (true) or F (false) beside each question:

1. I would not date a recently divorced or separated person. (T)(F)

2. I do not want an interracial or interfaith relationship. (T)(F)

3. My partner must meet my criteria physically (height, weight, etc). (T) (F)

4. My partner must be of a certain age group. (T)(F)

5. I would like my partner to be a college graduate or better. (T)(F)

6. I would like my partner to make a certain amount of money. (T) (F)

7. I want to avoid a partner with habits such as smoking, overeating, or sloppiness. (T)(F)

8. I want a partner who does not restrict my career, even temporarily. (T)(F)

9. I would avoid a relationship with someone who has children. (T)(F)

10. I would never go out with a person who was involved with someone else. (T) (F)

If you answered true to any of the questions, you are limiting yourself to a choice of partner. That's okay. Just so long as you know that you are inflexible in that area. If *all* your answers are true, perhaps you should consider broadening your view. In the long run, being open and flexible while choosing a partner is in your own best interest. For example, you might meet a terrific fellow who has some college experience, but not the degree. Would you be flexible enough to accept him?

What do you look for in a companion? Affection and romance? Companionship? Emotional security? Financial security? Power?

I'll bet if you have been single for a while, you have had plenty of time to make a long list in your head of all those characteristics your partner should have. In fact, I'm about to ask you to get your list out of your head and write it down on a piece of paper. But, before you do, take a look at my friend Dolores's list of desired traits for Mr. Perfect.

1. Good-looking
2. Taller than me
3. Slender or athletic-type body
4. Financially secure/upper income
5. A professional or businessman
6. College graduate/prefer a doctorate or masters
7. Likes golf and tennis and is better than I am
8. Hates football
9. Terrific lover
10. Sensitive and emotional
11. Very affectionate
12. Loves me deeply
13. Stable
14. Reliable
15. Trustworthy
16. Flexible and easygoing
17. Compassionate and understanding
18. Good sense of humor
19. Loves to dance
20. Loves to buy me flowers, clothes, presents
21. Eats everything - not fussy
22. Admired and respected by his colleagues

23. Popular with his patients/clients
24. Doesn't flirt
25. Likes my children and grandchildren
26. Loves to travel
27. Loves to eat out
28. Within five years of my age
29. Same religion
30. Has hair
31. Drives at night
32. Goes to church often

Now it's your turn. Find a sheet of paper and write down all the criteria you would like your special fella to have.

STEP THREE:

Okay, dear GG, it's time to get real. Your wish list is fantasy. No one man carries all the traits and characteristics that you have listed as your needs and wants. No one man is that perfect. But, of course, neither are we.

Even though sociologists say we look for partners who are similar to us in social background, education, age, interests, and intelligence, that's all well and good for our younger sisters. We are not only older, wiser, and more mature, we now outnumber our male counterparts almost four to one! We have to be realistic and reevalute these priorities.

I urge you at this point to modify your expectations and consider some vital factors, such as your appearance, age, financial status, past successes with men, how long you have been single, your lifestyle, and whether you are widowed or divorced.

In general, if you have power, and/or influence, and/or money, and/or you are above average in appearance, and/or are a professional (doctor, lawyer, etc.) and/or you have a talent, and/or you have a business - in other words, if you can bring something to the relationship that makes you stand out from others - you have every right, indeed, to look for a companion who will complement your lifestyle, talents, or profession. But, what if your lofty goals continue to lead to an empty heart and/or an empty bed?

If you are divorced, some men will have no interest in you because they have this strange idea that you must be to blame for the breakup and, therefore, you are faulty. It's an ugly reality but it's out there.

If you are in the your sixties or seventies and looking for a man your age, you know how slim the pickings are. Oftentimes, men your age are looking for younger gals to gratify their ego, i.e., make them feel younger. What is in your favor, however, is that once most of them have had a relationship or two, they begin to see the generation gap as a problem and some do become more realistic. For example, I was told recently by a seventy-two-year old man why he broke up with his former fifty-year old girlfriend. He had just finished having sex with this woman one evening and the time was 11:00 p.m. He wanted to stay in bed and sleep but she insisted on a midnight swim. That was last time he saw her.

If your income is modest and you are looking for a man to take care of you financially, it is a very hard quest to fulfill. Most men with money at this stage in their lives look for women who ask little of them financially. A man's monies are intended usually for his children and grandchildren.

If you have a Ph.D., you cannot be faulted for seeking an educated man. However, you may be hard-pressed to find even college graduates in your town. Perhaps you would be wise to expand your vision to a man with less than a college or graduate school degree. He may well be the best thing that's happened to you in years.

Let's get back to Dolores, whom I asked to do some re-evaluating, look over her list, and write down qualities that fulfilled fifty percent of her needs, not her desires. She thought long and hard, ten wrote:

1. Income equal to mine
2. Trustworthy
3. Stable and reliable
4. Affectionate
5. Good sense of humor
6. Compassionate and understanding
7. Likes my children
8. Enjoys sex
9. Loves me and wants a relationship or marriage

What a difference, wouldn't you say?

I'm now going to ask you to do the same.

Please sit down with your list and cross off all of your wants, leaving only your needs. Then return to your list and cross off 50 percent of your needs, leaving only the most important ones. Why? Because it's extremely hard to find men at this stage in your life, and I want you to widen your choices for finding the love of your life after fifty!

My friend, Evelyn, had been alone for fifteen years. She had a mammoth wish list about a potential partner. She had two or three lengthy relationships during that time but never could bring herself to settle down to a lifetime commitment because "no one was quite right."

She awoke one morning realizing that she did not want to be alone the rest of her life. Reevaluating her situation, she stopped looking for someone to fulfill her desires and thought more about her needs. Because her criteria became less strict, her social life became more active.

As time went on, she cut her list even more until it looked like this:

1. Financially secure
2. My religion
3. Plays golf (because she loved the sport and the lifestyle)

Of course, she enlarged her pool of candidates considerably. She had realized that she would automatically have no interest in a fellow who did not act gentlemanly, was not kind and considerate, was not trustworthy, and was not affectionate and warm. She allowed herself, then, to relax and enlarge her world to any number of men who could be likely partners.

Whom did she end up with? A very nice man.

In what ways did he fall short of her ideal partner? He was two inches shorter than she. He couldn't dance. He had no interest in travel unless he could play golf.

What did he do that she hadn't thought of? He did the dishes, made the bed, did all his own laundry, and turned out to be a much better housekeeper than she.

I have another girlfriend whose Significant Other has a fear of flying. She loves to fly. But, when they vacation, they drive, wherever it is. If she wants a cross-country trip by airplane or a European vacation, she travels without him. She compromised in order to have a companion in her life.

Another pal married a fellow who has a vacation home in the Hamptons. He told her after they were married that he didn't want overnight guests except for his children and grandchildren, because guests take away from relaxing with his family. The undesirables included *her* children and grandchildren. Accept it or stay in the city on weekends. She did accept it. Although she was not happy about it, she compromised in order to be in an otherwise happy relationship.

Perhaps if you were in their shoes, those types of compromises might well have been tough for you to make. Yet, did you not compromise when you first got married? Of course, you did. All good marriages are based on compromise.

I ask you to compromise again but this time with yourself. Know that is in your own best interest to shorten that list.

Please look at your list again. Cross off all of those needs that you recognize, down deep, are not really, truly important. Leave only those few that you cannot and will not compromise on.

List them here.

1. _____
2. _____
3. _____
4. _____
5. _____

Atta girl! I'm proud of you.

My sister and I sat in the theater at the end of Cinderella with tears streaming down our faces because we had believed in that story at one point in our lives, and, oh, the truth is **brutal.**
Miriam in "Flying Solo"
by Carol Anderson & Susan Stuart

7

ASSERT AND FLIRT TO MEET MEN

*If you think it's hard to meet new people,
just pick up the wrong golf ball.*

⊂⊃⊂⊃

If you are serious about meeting a companion, a future husband, a lover, or just dating once in a while, it is of considerable importance to put your imagination to work to *discover new and different ways to meet men*. That includes *being more assertive* than you probably are at this moment.

However, if you consider yourself an assertive person, feel free to skip this chapter. But before you leave, please take this word of advice. Most folks *avoid* overly assertive people. "Subtle" assertiveness is the topic we'll be addressing in this chapter.

I know being assertive was something that was always looked down on when we were in bobbysocks. If you were assertive and flirtatious, you knew how other gals felt about it, but you didn't care. To women for whom playing this game is natural, count yourself way ahead of those who are new at it.

Lorraine had a brother who owned a classic Corvette automobile. One day she asked her brother if she could borrow it for a week, not to drive it but just to let it sit in her driveway. He reluctantly agreed. She then placed an advertisement in the local newspaper listing the car for sale "for the best offer." She received over fifty phone calls, mostly from financially successful single men, the types who had enough disposable income to afford the purchase. Of course, they all wanted to see the car. And, of course, they had to meet her to see it. Seven of the prospective buyers asked her out on a date. As for the car, there was not one offer that was "acceptable" to Lorraine, as she had planned.

Did Lorraine take a risk? Most definitely. She risked having her ego bent out of shape if she attracted no suitors.

But aren't there always risks to every aspect of life? Are not romance and risk linked?

Your ability to take a risk, and perhaps rejection, has a big impact on how you feel about dating. But, if your life is going to change, you have to be the one to change it. As we age, we tend to narrow our world, and we can become invisible without trying to be. We also tend to be passive because we were accustomed, as young women, to being sought after.

Why not be assertive and do the choosing for a change? If you *don't* become assertive, your chances of meeting datable men are *slim*. Being creative, assertive, and flirtatious can bring new experiences to your life and new men into it.

Flirting, you say? "I've never flirted before, and I'm not going to start now."

Flirting is merely a form of communication. It makes people with whom you flirt feel good because you are paying attention to them. It is being friendly and directing one's conversation and body language to another person in order to begin a conversation, continue a conversation, and show that you are interested in that person.

Your inner voice says, "Nice girls don't flirt." *Not true.* Nice girls do flirt, particularly at this stage in their lives. Flirting means chatting with a man to determine whether you have a common ground on which to continue a conversation. Flirting is also entertaining. It's establishing verbal and non-verbal communication with another person. It's what's known as being "charming."

Women pay a big price by not choosing, by not being assertive. We have been conditioned to wait until we are chosen (being reactive) rather than taking the initiative and doing the choosing (being proactive).

The big secret we all would do well to learn - and which our younger sisters seem more skilled at (because they're gutsier than we are) - is how to capitalize on the moment. If you see an appealing man walking toward you or across a room, for example, rather than ignore him or wait for him to make the first move, you take the bull by the horns and do something.

ATTENDING A WORKSHOP

One dreary winter morning, as I was trudging through cold, wet, sleet-covered streets to the Boston Center for Adult Education, I wondered if the Guerrilla Dating Tactics workshop I was heading to would be worth it.

Excuse me? Guerrilla dating tactics?

Frankly, it was too good a learning experience to miss, especially to report on for single readers, and to satisfy my own curiosity. This day I was scheduled to gather information on how to attract and connect with new people while bringing fun and romance into one's life.

Arriving drenched and not fully convinced I should be there, I joined a large audience of mostly young, upscale professional types - with a larger-than-I-expected group of men - along with a sprinkling of Gorgeous Grandmas.

Honestly, I did not know what to expect. What with a discussion topic described in paramilitary terms, wouldn't you wonder about a certain crassness to the suggestions? Too, most of us are pretty comfortable in our skins and with what we know about worldly experiences. Even if we learned of other methods for meeting and behaving with the opposite sex, would we actually use them at this time in our lives? Would we, for example, be gutsy enough to send a note to a cute man across the room? Would we ask if a seat was taken next to a man *and then sit down in the man's lap*?

To my surprise, as the workshop progressed, I began to enjoy it, In fact, I came away with a lot more information than I had bargained for. For example, the word *guerrilla* in the title? It's merely to emphasize the resourcefulness and creativity of a guerrilla fighter, who uses whatever is on hand at the moment. Whenever you have no reason to talk with someone but really want to, you have to come up with a maneuver that is spontaneous, immediate, direct, and creative.

The expressions "If it's meant to be, it will happen" and "It'll happen when you're not looking" are jokes. They make little sense for a number of reasons, but above all, they make it too easy for you to be passive. Don't believe them.

WHAT ELSE DID I LEARN?

I learned that the first rule in dating is that there are no rules. Everyone is different; everyone's comfort level is different; there is no right way, no wrong way; the protocol is whatever you make it.

HOW TO BE MORE ASSERTIVE TOWARD THE OPPOSITE SEX

Here are some suggestions on what to do when opportunities present themselves:

* Drop some change as you walk by an interesting man. He will no doubt help you pick up your change, and you can start up a conversation.

* Ask for directions to a place toward which the man is walking, which gives you a chance to talk with him briefly. As you part, say you got to your destination so quickly because you enjoyed talking with him so much.

* If you see a man whom you wish to meet talking with others at a party - but you are leaving — take your business card and hand it to him with a written message: "I wish I had a chance to meet

you. I'd like to talk to you for a few minutes." Add your home phone number.

✳   If you see someone interesting at a store buying greeting cards, choose a funny card and show it to him.

✳   Take advantage of situations in which your man is a "captive audience" - waiting on a line, sitting on a bus, etc. Just start chatting. Ask some questions, but not too personal.

✳   Just pick up any piece of paper and ask him if he dropped it.

During a seminar I was presenting one day, a woman named Janet told our group her experience with being assertive. She was attending services in a synagogue on Friday night as part of a singles group. When the time came for the congregation to say a memorial prayer, those in the audience who had lost a dear one within the past year were invited to stand up and recite the special prayer. As Janet looked around, not one person started to stand. She decided to do so — even though she did not have a recently deceased relative — so that she could somehow be noticed at the mixer following the services. Janet stood up and recited the prayer with the rabbi. Did her courage pay off? You bet. She met some very nice men at the mixer.

ABOUT TAKING RISKS

Of course, assertive dating tactics are risky because you open yourself up to rejection. However, romance and risk are linked. Your ability to take risks will definitely impact your dating life. You have to make your interest known either directly or indirectly, in order to get the attention of the man.

As some women mature, they tend to camouflage themselves. They grow so ladylike and passive that often they are not even seen or noticed, which makes them feel that if no one picks them, they must not be worth picking. They need to make every effort to be assertive, dynamic, and self-confident, not passive.

I heard a story of a fellow who moved to a new apartment building with a pool. He complained that he went to the pool every Sunday for a month and not one of the many attractive women he admired there paid any attention to him as he read a book all afternoon. A friend suggested to him that he be more active and find a method of getting attention. The following Sunday, he appeared at the pool with a pitcher of Margaritas and sixteen glasses. He was alone no longer.

ABOUT ATTENDING AN EVENT ALONE

Most people feel anxious when attending a party or an event unescorted - or even with a friend. To calm that sense of foreboding, it's important to develop the right attitude.

* Begin by observing the crowd for ten to twenty minutes. Take some time to feel at ease. Smile a lot. Don't think about what you'll do next or even whom you'll talk to. You will probably feel comfortable in about thirty minutes.

* Don't think negatively - "Everyone looks awful." On the other hand, don't anticipate meeting the love of your life. Do anticipate the possibility of making a new friend. Continue to smile a lot.

* Start moving around the room. You can't meet anyone if you stand in a corner. You can't meet anyone if you sit in a chair. You can't meet more than one person if you cling to that person all night. You can't meet many people if you avert your eyes every time someone looks over at you.

ABOUT MOVING AWAY FROM AN UNINTERESTING PERSON

Speak for ten minutes with anyone who approaches you. If nothing clicks, move away graciously by saying: "Because I haven't been to a party in months"(or "Because I haven't had a date since Paul Newman got married"), I promised myself that I would circulate tonight. It was nice to meet you."

ABOUT FLIRTING

The ability to flirt goes hand in hand with the ability to take control of your life. Flirting with a man makes him feel good; it demonstrates that you appreciate his efforts and that you are giving a gift of yourself. Flirting should be fun. It is a form of communication. You are saying "I have a good feeling about you." When you flirt, you make things happen.

Of interest, Joyce Jillson, in her book, *The Fine Art of Flirting*, recommends "a woman must repeat a flirtatious gesture at least four or five times" so that the man can be sure she is interested in him. Too, a woman should "make bold, yet quick, gestures" for two or three seconds, then completely back off for three to five minutes before making another gesture. In order not to appear too bold, a woman needs to leave some time between each action. In other words, "overdo actions, overdo frequency, but don't overdo the time spent flirting."

Suggestions for Verbal Flirtations:
Say hello.
Use a low, sexy voice.
Compliment him.
Start a conversation.
Give him your phone number.
Tell him you've noticed him in the past.
Empathize.
Say his name as if you love the sound of it.

Suggestions for non-verbal flirtations:
Maintain eye contact.
Smile from the heart.
Wink.
Use body language.
Invade his space.
Establish some intrigue (share the moment).
Be attentive.
Be animated.
Be lively.
Send a note.
Send a drink.

SUGGESTIONS ON PLACES TO FLIRT:

Supermarket : Ask for his recipe for chicken or meatloaf.

On the street: Smile and say "hi"; walk your dog and bandage his tail to pique the interest of a passersby; or say "Hi, you look familiar."

Sightseeing: Ask him to take your picture or offer to take his.

In line: Compliment his clothes.

Cafe: Write in your journal or do a crossword puzzle, and ask him how to spell a word or help you think of an answer.

Office : Fax a valentine.

Parking lot : Ask about his car; leave a note on his windshield and be sure to sign your name.

Home: Chat on the internet.

Beach: Read a book with a provocative title to draw attention to it - and to you. Or read a computer magazine, aviation magazine, or other magazines that men might find interesting.

POSITIVE BODY LANGUAGE*

How to say "I like you" and how to tell if a man is interested in you.

* Direct eye contact (no staring)
* Warm, open smile
* Nodding
* Head tilted
* Open, inclusive gestures (palm showing)
* Fully facing you
* Leaning forward
* Upright but relaxed posture
* Firm handshake
* Double hand clasp handshake
* Feet firmly planted
* Chin up
* Sitting forward
* Touching another's arm or shoulder
* Winking (used with discretion)
* Tightened abdomen, sticking out chest
* Mirroring another's gestures and body stance
* "Accidentally" brushing another's hand
* Scanning the face wIth eyes
* Preening behavior: straightening tie, fixing hair, adjusting skirt, wetting lips
* Blocking behavior (to keep others away from the two of you)

*Adapted from: http://www.thirdage.com/romance/dating/quiz/ bodylanguage/tips.htm

NEGATIVE BODY LANGUAGE*

Are you guilty of this body language? Avoid these body movements and people will respond more positively towards you.

* Eye contact not met
* Tight expression or no smile
* Down and away glances
* Not fully facing the man, at an angle
* Leaning away
* Hunched shoulders
* Too-stiff posture
* Weak handshake
* Chin into chest
* Arms crossed
* Legs crossed
* Body sagging
* Legs outstretched when seated
* Absentminded gazes
* Dropped gazes
* Staring
* Fidgeting
* Standing too still
* Self-touching

Don't Waste Time on a Married Man

The problem with waiting for the perfect man to come into your life is that when he finally shows up, he has his wife with him.

A single friend of mine took a European vacation with a group. Upon her return, she told me about the trip and her traveling companions with great enthusiasm, mentioning some of the couples by name. I noticed she talked about one of the husbands a lot more than the rest.

When I asked her if something had happened between her and this fellow that I should know about (wink, wink), she laughed and said: "Of course not. He was just so-o-o nice, and he paid a lot more attention to me than some of the others on the trip. He even called me when I got home."

That, dear GGs, says it all: "He paid a lot more attention to me." For a woman alone - bottom line - there lies the allure of the married man.

It's lonely out there. I know it, and you know it. Your married girlfriends don't know it because they really don't know, down deep, what it is to be alone and lonely. Unhappy, maybe. Wanting to be alone sometimes, maybe. But all alone, all the time. Uh-uh. They really don't know.

Married men don't know what it is, either. However, certain married men - the cheatin' kind - think that many single (and married) gals are there just for the taking. And, they're right. Certain gals are there, just for the asking.

Look. I know it's tough. Intercourse is one activity we can't do by ourselves. We need a guy. And we need the flowers, the romance, the buildup, the cuddles, the kisses, the hugs, the foreplay, and the whole nine yards, perhaps as much as the physical act.

However, if a single gal has not been out on a date for a year and a half, can she forgive herself when she meets a married guy who comes on to her and they eventually make it to bed? Don't countless women know what it's like not to have had a physical relationship for even longer than that?

"What a tramp!" we would say about her. And, sure, he's a bum. He's betraying his marriage vows. But you know what? Neither he nor she cares what we think. They are simply interested in satisfying their mutual attraction.

There are certain women (single and married) who go out with married men. It's a disgusting fact of life, but it is life.

And, it's sad. Please feel sorry for the women (and men) who indulge in this stuff. I guess it's been going on forever, but it's not often thought about or talked about very much, except as gossip by nosy people. What is odd, however, is that those who cheat are often unaware of how many people know about it. And people do. It's almost impossible to keep matters of that sort private.

I am writing about this subject because I want to caution you, dear wonderful, perhaps lonely GG, to be aware of the dangers of fooling around with a married guy. What occurs is a great sex life (maybe) but a horrendous love life. Eventually, a self-indulgent but needy and loving woman is abandoned - after years, perhaps - of the part-time attention from "him" she's become accustomed to. I would think, if that's the case, isn't dating a married guy a waste of time to begin with?

What if he's promising to leave his wife for her? C'mon. It rarely happens. He will fade away discreetly, just after she expresses her need for more substance to their relationship than a roll-in-the-hay once a week.

My sixty-five-year-old friend, Roberta, is a perfect example. She met Bert on an airplane. He lived in Boston with his family, but because of his job he spent Monday through Friday in New York City, which is where Roberta lived.

For ten years, Roberta and Bert had a wild affair. He had money to burn and did. Limousines, caviar and champagne suppers, trips to London and Istanbul, flowers and love in the afternoon, exotic lingerie and other gifts.

At other times, she was alone. He missed her birthdays, their "meeting day" anniversaries, all national holidays, and even Valentine's Day.

Of course. What do we expect? Isn't that the life of "the other woman?"

Except for one thing. Roberta should not have been the other woman. She was a highly respected professional in her own right, with a great job, exciting travel life, and a beautiful apartment. She was a mover and shaker in her world and a terrific gal to boot. An intelligent woman, Roberta ended up acting like a big dummy. Why? She was fifty-five when she met Bert, and suddenly it was ten years later. If she had walked away from the airport that night and out of this married man's life, she would have remained open and available for other relationships. When she became entirely focused on her clandestine trysts, she removed herself from all opportunities to meet an available, first-class, single guy who could have been hers for the rest of her life!

I heard from Roberta a while back. She was feeling depressed and lonely. Bert's wife had died and Roberta had hoped beyond all hope that she would be his second one. It didn't happen. Bert dropped her shortly after his wife's funeral. Roberta saw his photograph in the newspaper from time to time. He appeared to be dating younger and/or wealthier women.

More about a "no-win" situation in a letter from a reader of my column:

Dear Gorgeous Grandma:

A number of years ago, I began an affair with a married man. I knew it was wrong and it took me a while to admit to myself that even though I was physically satisfied, I was acting like a tramp. But, I didn't care. Because I was single, lonely, and yearning for love, I became a fool.

I saw the man for eight or so years two or three times a month. He had told me at the outset that he would never divorce his wife. I didn't care. I felt that I would continue our relationship until I met someone important to me, and then I would stop seeing Elliot. In fact, I would use him as he was using me.

I did not realize, however, how much our evenings together would mean to me. I fell in love with Elliot and it soon happened that every man I met I would compare and, subsequently, set aside because of my feelings for Elliot.

A few years ago, Elliot's wife died. Wow, I thought. There's a real future for us. But, I was wrong. Elliot faded from my life. Within six months, I no longer heard from him. I was certainly getting a message.

I finally got over him and began seeking another life. I started dating again and met a few nice men. Finally, I found my man and I am married again (I'm 71).

However, my dilemma. Along the way, I had invested in Elliot's business and, from time to time, I am required to speak to him directly. I must admit that, very recently, I had lunch with him and it was like old times. He tells me he loves dating (he's 76) and that he will probably never marry again. But, he has been seeing one woman on a steady basis for more than a year.

Yet, he told me how attracted he is to me still, and how he would love to go to bed with me; plus he described to me over lunch what he would like to do in bed. I told him that I did not like him talking to me that way and that I could not renew our friendship, *even on a business basis, if he continued to talk to me in that manner.*

Last week, I was required to call him again about business. He told me about his recent vacation (without his steady) and what a wonderful time he had meeting other women. He then began to talk dirty to me over the phone and I told him to to stop it. He then told me that I had changed; that I am dried-up old woman and that I have become sexless. I hung up the phone.

I feel so hurt and sad about this man. I would love to maintain our friendship as I valued his advice and caring over the years. I think I still need that. How, though, can I continue on my terms instead of his?

Gloria T., Providence, R.I.

This was my response.

Dear Gloria;

Common sense tells us (as well as research and my conversations with a vast number of single GGs) that a relationship with a married man is, in general, a losing game. There are some women who do end up with the target of their affection but, their numbers are minuscule compared to the losers.

What does surprise me, however, is that most women did not regret their "married man experience;" in fact, most felt they had benefited and learned a lot from that relationship.

Nevertheless, I don't think your relationship with Elliot was ever on your terms. You would like to believe it was because it's important to feel, somehow, in control. But your "yearning for love" was your downfall. Your vulnerability blinded you. Sometimes it's tough to think with what's behind our eyes instead of with what's above our thighs. It does help to ask, however, "Is it worth it?"

When a relationship is generated by sexual attraction solely - and, in most cases, what else does a married man want - isn't that relationship destined to remain on a sexual level forever? Dating normally, we would be fools to hop into bed with a man without knowing him very, very well. Consequently, when a romance moves to the intimate stage, we have a foundation of attraction, mutual interests, trust, respect, and all kinds of nice things solidly established (I like to think) before intimacy enters the picture.

On the other hand, when a clandestine affair is under-way, sex is, generally, the sole motivation for the man. All the wonderful attributes you have, as the person you are, merely go along for the ride.

A married man who has an affair is not only a "rogue" or a "you devil you" as his friends might say affectionately, with even a bit of envy. He is a cheat, a philanderer, and not to be trusted. Elliot is a user and, indeed, still a philanderer. Didn't he cheat on his girlfriend when away on vacation?

Elliot is using you, through his sex talk, to get a spur-of-the-moment high. And do ignore his "you're sexless" putdown. He's angry because you have rejected him. But he will keep using you as long as you let him! You may think you need him for whatever emotional support may be missing from your marriage. I'll bet, though, at this stage in your life, you can stand on your own two feet quite well.

I want to encourage you to remove Elliot from your life as quickly as possible. If your business with him requires con-versation, have someone else do it - a lawyer, an accountant, your husband. Turn your weakness about him into a strength and stay away. Your attempt to remain friends demonstrates that you still care for him even though he dumped you after he became a widower. Where is your self-respect, girl?

Think hard about why you still want him in your life. Is he worth it?

I think not.

Think hard about your husband and your relationship with him. Is he worth it?

I would hope so.

Here is a bit of advice from the well-known entertainer Diahann Carroll. She waited eighteen years (from 1958 to 1976) for actor Sidney Poitier to leave his first wife. It never happened.

> *"I became slavishly devoted to Sidney. It took me nine years to realize he was just having a sexual affair with me while still enjoying all the comforts of married life. When I hear of women having affairs with married men and giving up their self-esteem and independence, I want to tell all of them: 'Dump the bum!' Don't let yourself be used. It's not worth the heartache."*

And how's this for an interesting turn of events. The television show, *20/20*, reported that a North Carolina housewife sued "the other woman" for entrapment in an "alienation of affection" suit. The jury awarded $1 million to the rejected wife. Even though it will be difficult to collect because the newly married couple is unstable financially, there is something to be said, indeed, for a successful and perhaps profitable revenge.

CONCLUSION

THIS INSIDER'S POINT OF VIEW

Sometimes I wonder if men and women really suit each other.
Perhaps they should live next door and just visit now and then.
                                                    Katherine Hepburn

The purpose of this book, dear GGs, has been to inspire, motivate, and encourage you to move forward in your life in order to find a fine man to put in it. That quest is not an easy one.

Many of you at midlife have created a personal world that may well be fulfilling and rich without a companion. Even though you know what you want from a relationship and the ways intimacy can enhance your life, you know how much time it takes to maintain a relationship, and you know you don't want to settle. Perhaps, for these reasons, you haven't taken the time or made the effort to find a suitable partner.

In their book *Flying Solo: Single Women in Midlife*, Carole Anderson, Susan Stewart, and Sona Dimidjian explain that there are three reasons why midlife women are reluctant to "throw themselves into a full-scale search for their ideal relationship: (the) gender lag, the all too predictable consequences of the urge to merge, and the depressing nature of the dating scene."

The "gender lag" refers to the assumptions that midlife men make about being "the center of a woman's whole existence. They assume that women will accommodate their schedules and their needs." In fact, many of the women the authors interviewed found *few* men interested in them because of their independence. The authors explain:

> "Today's women have chosen to redefine and expand their notions of what it means to be female and what it means to have a relationship with a man. These ideas often directly contradict the values of the marriage and motherhood mandate, which dictate that women should *always* and *unconditionally* desire to be in a relationship - no matter what. Having adapted to the enormous cultural changes that have occurred in

the short space of their own lifetime, modern women find they are out of sync with most of the men they meet . . . . No matter what they say they want in personal ads, few midlife men are really ready to join their female counterparts on the cusp of cultural change. Their expectations remain anchored in a couple of time zones behind the expectations of these women."

While most of us formerly dependent women have grown to depend finally on ourselves and have tried to put certain behaviors behind us, most of our male counterparts have been conditioned to expect them still.

These expectations may well be why some midlife men are attracted to younger women. Younger women are viewed as being more flexible and more willing to defer to an older man's experience. Those men who attract younger women believe that by having done so means they aren't old and their body parts haven't died, However, in certain circles, it has as much to do with the younger woman's quest for financial security as it does with the man's youthfulness or attractiveness.

Reluctance on the part of midlife women to seek relationships is also the result of the fear women have of returning to a "need to please." They fear reverting to their childhood expectation that it's the woman's job to accommodate, which results in her needs not being taken seriously. Hence, women are reluctant to chance the dating scene in midlife because of a worry that they may adopt a position of selflessness.

"They worry that, in the heat of the passionate first stages of an intimate relationship, they will give up, little by little, all they have learned, all the freedoms they have fought for and achieved in the years on their own. These women fear their own tendencies to revert to 'automatic pilot,' to accommodate and defer, eventually metamorphosing into some stranger they hardly recognize and certainly don't like."

The authors maintain that the third reason midlife women stay away from the dating scene is that it's "boring, time-consuming and even humiliating. These women are not willing to put themselves through degrading experiences when they have attained the all-important feeling of being complete and capable on their own." To further explain these women's lack of interest, ". . . midlife women were taught to be passive, to wait patiently to be *found* rather than to *seek out* what they want . . . . It does not feel natural for them to pursue a relationship aggressively."

Sandi explains:

> *I always fantasized that a relationship would just fall into my lap. You know, here I am working in this setting with interesting men, educated people and all of our contacts . . . . But it just doesn't happen. So I've got to put myself out there, which takes work and a commitment of time. I have to push myself past my comfort level again.*

Perhaps you, too, have chosen not to enter the dating world because of these excuses. Your reluctance about stepping out to bring a man into your life is well understood. However, my hope is that you have now changed your mind - that you found the chapters you have read, the recommendations that were made, and the self-exploration quizzes you took, a valuable and rewarding experience.

I believe it is important to recognize that contrary to the opinions we have just discussed, compromise is a fact of life. In order to make our way in this world, men and women both have used compromise *ad infinitum*, beginning with childhood negotiations with our parents up to learning to get along with our daughters- or sons-in-law. As a wife, mother, and now a significant other, I did not, and still do not, consider accommodating my loved ones to be degrading or negative. In fact, I have often been on the receiving end of "accommodation" over the years, and I'll bet you have, too.

As for fearing my "need to please", I, for one, have no fear. If I feel like making my significant other happy, my children happy, my friends happy, I do so without reluctance or worry that I am being subservient, subordinate, or too eager to please. I am fulfilling my wish to express myself in that manner.

What about their description of the "depressing nature of the dating scene." I can't agree to that view at all. If we all thought about dating in such a negative manner, where would our second marriages have sprung from? What would happen to those of us who like and/or love men, have been married, divorced, or single up to our mid-years, and want to have a loving relationship in our lives? It's much too defeating a thought for our purposes. **Indeed, we are *not seeking* a life in the dating scene; we are *using* the dating scene to find the love of our life.**

Yes, acquiring the thoughts and actions to be successful at finding a partner *can* take time and *does* require work. However, if you choose to use the information that I have researched and experienced in this book, if you do take the time to put it into action, and you do work at it to find a serious love interest, you *can* be successful in your quest.

Let us now review those eight important components that will bring you success in finding the love of your life after fifty!

Dating is different at this age. It's different because our expectations and goals have changed. Perhaps companionship is more important now than lust; perhaps cuddling is more fun at times than sex. Perhaps dating might be confusing or disappointing as well as that awful fear of being rejected. There are those unexpected conflicts adjusting to children's agendas should you become serious with a man. Too, there's a bit (or a lot) of baggage we (or he) bring(s) to a relationship. Know, though, that you're not alone Plan to take one step at a time, learn to gain control over the small things, seek a pal to talk to, if need be, and absolutely, positively make new friends.

Get out and about to meet men. You cannot sit home and hope that somehow, someway, a nice guy will find out about you and want to meet you. A lot of energy and effort has to be expended in order to develop a social life. Take from one who knows - you have to kiss at least a few frogs! There is no shortcut, unless you do something foolish like attach yourself to the first fellow you meet because you can't bear to be single. Get up, get out, and get going! You're future lover is waiting for you!

Find lots of dates in cyberspace. If you haven't become computer-savvy, now is a good time to do it. Find yourself a good computer school and take a class. Not only will the Internet keep you contemporary with all the men your age who use it, but you might very well find the love of your life there.

Looking great will attract those dates. Even if you don't have movie-star looks, you can still be a stunner and top-notch on the well-groomed list. Give yourself a beauty checkup and, as my son reminded me often, "Get your act together!" Men are visual creatures and the better the package, the more appealing you become. Not that he won't love you for your brains. He'll discover them, too, eventually.

Be adaptable enough to risk new adventures. It's in your own best interest to be less judgmental, more forgiving, and easier to please. When you expand your friendship base by being open and amenable to different personalities and types of men than you've been acquainted with in the past, friendship, companionship, love, and romance will be yours. Do try something new!

Be realistic about men. Identify the type of man you think need and then shorten the list. When you recognize that Prince Charming doesn't exist, you will probably find many more men in your life than you can handle!

Be assertive and flirt to meet men. It's really tough to be bold. However, if you don't take the bull by the horns and start choosing, instead of waiting on the sidelines to be chosen, time and men may pass you by. Learn to flirt or, at the very least, learn to recognize when a man is flirting with you!

Don't waste your time with a married man. Loneliness can make a woman weak and available to the charms of a philanderer. Don't allow his attentiveness to conquer your good sense.

It has been a pleasure and a delight sharing with you all that I learned, researched, and experienced over the many years as a single. Now that I am one-half of a couple, do know that this pairing occurred only as a result of my listening to my own advice.

I wish you luck, love, and much happiness in your life, whether you choose to continue in the single life or not. Just remember, you are the sole mistress of your fate. If you choose to seek happiness with a man, I know you can bring love and romance back into your life. Why? Because after twenty-five years of marriage and, subsequently, fifteen years alone, I did.

Appendix A
More Self-Help
Quizzes

GENERAL LIFESTYLE ANALYSIS*

The following questions have been formulated to offer you a general view of who you are, which will assist you in identifying your adaptability to others as well as your wants and needs in a relationship.

1. Are you more organized or more spontaneous?

    _____
    _____

2. Are you a very neat housekeeper, who cleans regularly and thoroughly, or are you sloppy and haphazard about it? Do you pay someone else to do it for you?

    _____
    _____

3. Do you like a busy-looking home, with lots of stuff on the walls and knickknacks and mementos on the table and shelves? Or, do you prefer a spare, clean, uncluttered environment? Do you like decorative frills or straight clean lines? Contempary or Victorian?

    _____
    _____
    _____

4. Are you around people a lot by choice?

    _____
    _____

5. Do you spend more time with your girlfriends, with men, or with mixed groups? With one person at a time, or several? With old friends, family, new acquaintances, your children, former lovers?

    _____
    _____
    _____

6. Do you spend much time alone? Do you like solitude?

    _____
    _____
    _____

*Adapted from *The Unofficial Guide to Dating Again* by Tina Tessina, Ph.D. MacMillan General Reference, NY, 1998, p.113.

7. Do you have pets? How much of your time do you spend with them? Will a partner have to like pets, too?

    _____

    _____

    _____

8. Do you have children and grandchildren? Do they live with you, either full or part-time? How often are they around? How close are you to them?

    _____

    _____

    _____

9. Are you artistic? Do you often have a creative project going? Do you spend a lot of time at it?

    _____

    _____

10. Do you have a sport or hobby that consumes lots of time, energy, and/or money?

    _____

11. How are you with money? Are you responsible? Are you very detailed or more casual? For example, do you balance your checkbook every month, to the penny, or do you get a vague idea of how much you have left from the deposit receipt? Do you ever bounce checks? Are you meticulous about paying bills or do you sometimes get late charges? Do you like doing the accounting chores (paying bills, balancing checkbook) or do you wish someone else would do it?

    _____

    _____

12. Is food important to you? Do you like to cook? To entertain? To dine out? Do you follow a special or vegetarian diet?

    _____

    _____

13. Do you like intense conversation? What about?

    _____

    _____

14. Are you careful or casual about your appearance?

    _____

15. Are you spiritual or religious? Do you attend a church, synagogue, temple, retreats, or meditation sessions?

_____

_____

16. Are you comfortable with your tried and true habits, or do you like to change the routine from from time to time?

_____

_____

_____

ARE YOU READY FOR A RELATIONSHIP?
FIVE-PART QUESTIONNAIRE

QUIZ #1
GENERAL ATTITUDE

1. Place a checkmark on the left side of every statement that you believe applies to you. Leave all statements blank that do not apply to you.

_____ I first need to know myself before I reach out for a meaningful relationship. (A) _____

_____ I'm not perfect but for some reason I keep looking for the perfect relationship (B) _____

_____ I'm bored being alone. (B) _____

_____ If we're not the same religion, the relationship doesn't seem to last. (B) _____

_____ I am looking for a mate who will rescue me from my own personal problems. (C) _____

_____ I am no good alone. I need someone to take care of me. (C) _____

_____ It is important that I treat my lover as my best friend. (A) _____

_____ Financial security is everything to me and it is what I am looking for in a partner even if I don't feel like I'm in love. (C) _____

_____ Finding love doesn't come automatically. It takes a concrete plan. (A) ___A___

_____ Love can begin with a chance meeting but won't develop without nurture. (B) ___B___

_____ I do not want a lifetime mate. (C) _____

*from *Love & Sex Tests* by Louis Janda, Ph.D., Adams Media Corp.,Holbrook, MA., p.4

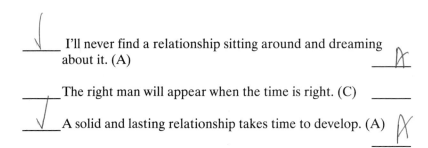

_____ I'll never find a relationship sitting around and dreaming about it. (A)

_____ The right man will appear when the time is right. (C)

_____ A solid and lasting relationship takes time to develop. (A)

2. Return to question #1. Place A, B, or C on the right of each statement that you've checked.

3. Add how many A's in the column and fill in the blank below. Add how many B's in your column and fill in the blank below. Do the same for C's.

Total (A) _3_ x 1= _3_
Total (B) _1_ x 2= _2_
Total (C) ___ x 3= ___
Total quiz #1= _5_

Quiz #2
WORK WORLD vs. PERSONAL LIFE

1. Place a checkmark on the left side of every statement that you believe applies to you. Leave all statements blank that do not apply to you.

_____ I am so exhausted by the end of the day that all I want to do is curl up with a good book and go to bed early. (C) _____

_____ Right now work is my priority. (C) _____

_____ My work is very isolating and I get "people starved." I try to go out and socialize as much as possible. (B) _____

_____ Between my job and my friends, I have all the loving relationships I need. (C) _____

_____ I spend as much time working on finding a relationship as I do on my work activities. (A) _____

_____ I deal with so many people each day that my idea of a perfect evening is sitting home alone with a drink in one hand and my TV remote in the other. (C) _____

____✓____ I would be willing to change jobs or even relocate if the right relationship came along. (A) ___A___

_____ I work so hard just trying to survive that "working" on a relationship is more than I could bear right now. (C) _____

___✓___ The perfecting ending to the day would be to come home to that very special someone. (A) ___A___

_____ My main "ambition" in life is to find a lasting relationship. (A) _____

2. Return to question #1. Place A, B, or C on the right of each statement that you've checked.

3. Add how many A's in the column and fill in the blank below. Add how many B's in your column and fill in the blank below. Do the same for C's.

Total (A) _2_ x 1=_2_

Total (B)____ x 2= ____

Total (C)____ x 3= ____

Total quiz #2 = _2_

Quiz #3
RELATIONSHIPS

1. Place a checkmark on the left side of every statement that you believe applies to you. Leave all statements blank that do not apply to you.

_____ Love has been too painful in the past so I will settle for a relationship of convenience. (C) _____

_____ I have found that I am not a full person without that special someone in my life. (B) _____

___✓___ I am willing to take a serious look at what went wrong in my last relationship and how I could have made it better. (A)

_____

_____ My husband and I split up. I don't know where or how to begin to find a new relationship. (C) _____

_____ I am not willing to set myself up for another rejection. (C)

_____

_____ All the men I go out with want sex, but none of them seem to want a permanent relationship. (C) _____

_____ I spent most of my time raising the children alone and now that they are all gone, my life seems empty. I've almost forgotten how to socialize with adults. (B) _____

_____ My own identity has been a little shaken by a failed relationship, so I want to get my act together before looking for another one. (B) _____

_____ After dating so many men, I know exactly what I am looking for. (B) _____

_____ I am alone because no one cares. (C) _____

_____ My husband recently died, and I'm trying to get my life back in order. (B) _____

_____ The only way that I feel like a whole person is in contact with another. (B)   _____

_____ My last relationship ended so miserably that I'm afraid to try another one so soon. (B)   _____

_____ I am alone because I just never found the right man. (B)

_____

_____ I've never really sat down and made a list of qualities I am looking for in a mate. (C)   _____

___✓___ I've been alone and happy with myself. I only want a relationship if it can add new and lovely dimensions to my life. (A)   _A___

_____ I am a very busy person. Another person would have to fit into my schedule. (B)   _____

2. Return to question #1. Place A, B, or C on the right of each statement that you've checked.

3. Add how many A's in the column and fill in the blank below. Add how many B's in your column and fill in the blank below. Do the same for C's.

Total (A) _1_ x 1=____

Total (B)____x 2= ____

Total (C)____x 3=____

Total quiz #3= _1_

Quiz #4
PRESSURE FROM SELF/FAMILY/ FRIENDS

1. Place a checkmark on the left side of every statement that you believe applies to you. Leave all statements blank that do not apply to you.

_____ My relatives keep asking me, "When are you going to get married?" They won't get off my back until I do. (C) _____

_____ All my friends are married and I feel left out. (C) _____

_____ I am desperate for a relationship before it gets too late. (C) _____

__✓__ It's never too late to find a relationship and I'm never too old to stop looking. (A) __4__

_____ My idea of a perfect mate is someone just like the man I was married to. (C) _____

_____ I won't find a partner willing to take me and my children as his responsibility. (C) _____

_____ My friends think I am nobody since I don't have a serious relationship. (C) _____

_____ It doesn't matter what my family or my friends think. It's my life and my relationship and I'll take my time. (A) _____

__✓__ It's okay to be alone but it would be better if I could find that other person who wants love as much as I do. (A) __A__

_____ I need to spend a lot of time with my family/friends. (C) _____

_____ I couldn't possibly fall in love with someone of a different background (religion or race). (C) _____

_____ I'd consider anyone of any background who met my general values. (A) _____

___✓___ Education means a lot to me. Someone of a lesser status would make me feel uncomfortable. (B)   ___A___

_____ I don't mind what a person does for a living so long as he is nice and decent and we have things in common. (A)   _____

2. Return to question #1. Place A, B, or C on the right of each statement that you've checked.

3. Add how many A's in the column and fill in the blank below. Add how many B's in your column and fill in the blank below. Do the same for C's.

Total (A)_3_ x 1=_3_____

Total (B)____x 2= _____

Total (C)____x 3= _____

Total quiz #4= _3____

Quiz #5
HEALTH/FINANCES/ACTIVITIES

1. Place a checkmark on the left side of every statement that you believe applies to you. Leave all statements blank that do not apply to you.

_____ I am not physically fit and I don't feel good about myself. (C)

_____

✓ I take care of myself and am sure I get the proper nutrition, exercise, and sleep. (A)

_____

_____ Even if I have to skip a few meals, I am sure to save money for my hair and nails, plus enough for weekly entertainment. (A)

_____

_____ I don't go anywhere unless I look my best. (A)

_____

_____ I always intend to get dressed up and go out over the weekend but I usually end up sitting at home in my jeans or sweats. (C)

_____

_____ I always wear clothes that emphasize my best physical features and ones that reflect my personality. (A)

_____

_____ I'm not very adventurous and I'm afraid to take chances. Meeting new people is not comfortable so I don't go out. (C)

_____

_____ I meet a few people, give them my number, and then stay home waiting for the phone to ring. (B)

_____

_____ Each week one of my favorite pastimes is to figure out creative new places and new ways to meet men. (A)

_____

_____ I'm so sick of bars, and those are the only places you can meet men. (C)

_____

_____ I am not willing to change myself for a relationship. Someone will love me despite my looks. (C)

_____

_____ I am willing to take as much time and spend as much money as it takes to find the perfect relationship. (A) _____

_____ There are a number of things I like to do alone. (B) _____

_____ I hate doing things alone. (C) _____

_____ My after-work activities take up most of my spare time. (B)
_____

_____ I wouldn't consider anyone who is not in my own financial bracket. (C) _____

_____ It's important to me that my partner and I share an interest in the same activities and sports. (B) _____

2. Return to question #1. Place A, B, or C on the right of each statement that you've checked.

3. Add how many A's in the column and fill in the blank below. Add how many B's in your column and fill in the blank below. Do the same for C's.

Total (A)_1_ x 1=_1_

Total (B)___x 2= ____

Total (C)___x 3= ____

Total quiz #5 _1_

KEY TOTALS

Totals:

Test #1   5

Test #2   2

Test #3   1

Test #4   3

Test #5   1

_____ 12 **Overall Total**

EVALUATION:

1. If you scored 25 or less, you are ready and willing to welcome a new and special someone into your life.

2. If you scored between 25 - 55, you might well be ready for a relationship, but it would be wise for you to re-evaluate and review the priorities you have chosen to follow in your life.

3. If you scored 55 or more, the present time is not the best time for you to enter into a relationship.

LONELINESS*

Are you lonely? Or do you enjoy being alone most of the time?

The following statements reflect people's feelings about loneliness. Indicate how often you feel that way by writing a number in the space provided. For example, in answer to the question "How often do you feel happy?" you would respond with a 1, indicating "never," if you never feel happy. If you always feel happy, you would respond with a 4, indicating "always."

Never = 1
Rarely =2
Sometimes = 3
Always = 4

2 _2_ 1. How often do you feel that you are "in tune" with the people around you?

_3_ 2. How often do you feel that you lack companionship?

_1_ 3. How often do you feel that there is no one you can turn to?

_3_ 4. How often do you feel alone?

3 _2_ 5. How often do you feel part of a group of friends?

3 _2_ 6. How often do you feel that you have a lot in common with the people around you?

_1_ 7. How often do you feel that you are no longer close to anyone?

_3_ 8. How often do you feel that your interests and ideas are not shared by those around you?

2 _3_ 9. How often do you feel outgoing and friendly?

1 _4_ 10. How often do you feel close to people?

_3_ 11. How often do you feel left out?

*Adapted from *Modern Maturity* magazine, Nov-Dec 1999, p.33. Quiz developed by Harvard Medical School researchers, Thomas Perls, M.D. and Margery Hutter Silver, Ed.D., to help calculate estimated life expectancy.

___1___ 12. How often do you feel that your relationships with others are not meaningful?

___1___ 13. How often do you feel that no one really knows you well?

___3___ 14. How often do you feel isolated from others?

2. ___3___ 15. How often do you feel you can find companionship when you want it?

1. ___4___ 16. How often do you feel that there are people who really understand you?

___3___ 17. How often do you feel shy?

___3___ 18. How often do you feel that people are around you but not with you?

2 ___2___ 19. How often do you feel that there are people you can talk to?

1. ___4___ 20. How often do you feel that there are people you can turn to?

17   42

∞∞

SCORING

1. Before adding your total score, please change your answers in the following manner:

If your answer to Question #1 was 1, change it to 4
2, change it to 3
3, change it to 2
4, change it to 1

2. Do the same changes for Questions #5,#6, #9, #10, #15, #16, #19, and #20. The purpose of these changes is to adjust your score for a correct evaluation.

3. Total your revised score. _____42_____ Total

LONELINESS QUIZ RESULTS

Low scores indicate less loneliness. High scores indicate greater loneliness.

If you received a score of 49, for example, it means that 70 percent of people scored lower than you did in the level of loneliness.

	Score	Percentile
LOW LEVEL OF LONELINESS	31	15
	36	30
MEDIUM LEVEL OF LONELINESS	40	50
	44	70
HIGH LEVEL OF LONELINESS	49	85

It is in your best interest not begin a romantic relationship if you are feeling lonely. Attempting to fill the emptiness in your life by finding a companion will not be the answer. When you feel good about yourself and your life, a relationship will have a much better chance of succeeding.

LONGEVITY QUIZ*
WILL YOU LIVE TO BE 100?

<u>Score</u>

1. Do you smoke or chew tobacco, or are you around a lot of secondhand smoke? Yes (-20) No (0)   _O_

2. Do you cook your fish, poultry, or meat until it is charred? Yes (-2) No (0)   _O_

3. Do you avoid butter, cream, pastries, and other saturated fats as well as fried foods? Yes (+3) No (-7)   _+3_

4. Do you minimize meat in your diet, preferably making a point of eating plenty of fruits, vegetables, and whole grains instead? Yes (+5) No (-4)   _+5_

5. Do you consume more than two drinks of beer, wine, and/or liquor a day? (A standard drink is one 12-ounce bottle of beer, one wine cooler, one five-ounce glass of wine, or one and a half ounces of 80-proof distilled spirits.) Yes (-10) No (0)   _O_

6. Do you drink beer, wine, and/or liquor in moderate amounts (one or two drinks/day)? Yes (+3) No (0) _O_

7. Do air pollution warnings occur where you live? Yes (-4) No (+1)   _-4_

8. (a) Do you drink more than 16 ounces of coffee a day? Yes (-3) No (0) _O_
   (b) Do you drink tea daily? Yes (+3) No (0)   _3_

9. Do you take an aspirin a day? Yes (+4) No (0)   _O_

10. Do you floss your teeth every day? Yes (+2) No (-4) _+2_

11. Do you have a bowel movement less frequently than once every two days? Yes (-4) No (0)   _O_

12. Have you had a stroke or heart attack? Yes (-10) No (0) _O_

* Adapted from *Living to 100: Lesson in Living to Your Maximum Potential at Any Age* (New York: Basic Books, 1999) by Thomas Perls, MD and Margery Hutter Silver, Ed.D., with John F. Lauerman.

13. Do you try to get a suntan? Yes (-4) No (+3)   *+3*

14. Are you more than 20 pounds overweight?
    Yes (-10) No (0)   *0*

15. Do you live near enough other family members
    (other than your spouse and dependent children)
    that you can and want to drop in on spontaneously?
    Yes (+5) No (-4)   *-4*

16. Which statement applies to you? (a) "Stress eats away
    at me. I can't seem to shake it off." Yes (-7) or (b)"I
    can shed stress." This might be by prayer, exercise,
    meditation, finding humor in everyday life, or other
    means. Yes (+7)   *+7*

17. Did both of your parents either die before age 75 of
    nonaccidental causes or require daily assistance by
    the time they reached age 75? Yes (-10) No (0)   *0*

18. Did more than one of the following relatives live to
    at least age 90 in excellent health: parents, aunts/uncles,
    grandparents? Yes (+24) No (0) I don't know (0)   *0*

19. (a) Are you a couch potato (do no regular aerobic or
    resistance exercise)? Yes (-7) or (b) Do you exercise
    at least three times a week? Yes (+7)   *+7*

20. Do you take vitamin E (400-800 IU) and selenium
    (100-200 mcg) every day? Yes (+5) No (-3)   *+5*

SCORE:

27

5

5 | 27

Step 1: (a) Add the negative and positive scores together.
        Example: -45 plus +30 = -15.
     (b) Divide the preceding score by 5
        (-15 divided by 5 = -3)

Step 2: Add the negative or positive number to age 84 if you are a
        man or
        Add the negative or positive number to age 88 if you are a
        woman
        (example: -3 + 88 = 85) to get your estimated life span.

THE SCIENCE BEHIND THE LONGEVITY QUIZ*

Question 1: Cigarette smoke contains toxins that directly damage DNA, causing cancer and other diseases and accelerating aging.

Question 2: Charring food changes its proteins and amino acids into heterocyclic amines, which are potent mutagens that can alter your DNA.

Questions 3, 4: A high-fat diet, and especially a high-fat, high-protein diet, may increase your risk of cancer of the breast, uterus, prostate, colon, pancreas, and kidney. A diet rich in fruits and vegetables may lower the risk of heart disease and cancer.

Questions 5, 6: Excessive alcohol consumption can damage the liver and other organs, leading to accelerated aging and increased susceptibility to disease. Moderate consumption may lower the risk of heart disease.

Question 7: Certain air pollutants may cause cancer; many also contain oxidants that accelerate aging.

Question 8: Too much coffee predisposes the stomach to ulcers and chronic inflammation, which in turn raise the risk of heart disease. High coffee consumption may also indicate and exacerbate stress. Tea, on the other hand, is noted for its significant antioxidant content.

Question 9: Taking 81 milligrams of aspirin a day (the amount in one baby aspirin) has been shown to decrease the risk of heart disease, possibly because of its anticlotting effects.

Question 10: Research now shows that chronic gum disease can lead to the release of bacteria into the bloodstream, contributing to heart disease.

Question 11: Scientists believe that having at least one bowel movement every 20 hours decreases the incidence of colon cancer.

Question 12: A previous history of stroke and heart attack makes you more susceptible to future attacks.

Question 13: The ultraviolet rays in sunlight directly damage DNA, causing wrinkles and increasing the risk of skin cancer.

---

* Adapted from *Living to 100: Lesson in Living to Your Maximum Potential at Any Age* (New York: Basic Books, 1999) by Thomas Perls, MD and Margery Hutter Silver, Ed.D., with John F. Lauerman.

Question 14: Being obese increases the risk of various cancers, heart disease, and diabetes. The more overweight you are, the higher your risk of disease and death.

Questions 15, 16: People who do not belong to cohesive families have fewer coping resources and therefore have increased levels of social and psychological stress. Stress is associated with heart disease and some cancers.

Questions, 17, 18: Studies show that genetics plays a significant role in the ability to reach old age.

Question 19: Exercise leads to more efficient energy production in the cells and overall less oxygen radical formation. Oxygen (or free) radicals are highly reactive molecules or atoms that damage cells and DNA, ultimately leading to aging.

Question 20: Vitamin E is a powerful antioxidant and has been shown to retard the progress of Alzheimer's, heart disease, and stroke. Selenium may prevent some types of cancer.

Please keep in touch!

Dear Gorgeous Grandma ~

It has been a treat for me to have had this opportunity to encourage you to find a companion to share life with, as well as to share with you a number of stories about our different, funny, and sometimes outrageous single life. But it has been a one-way conversation up to this point.

Now I would love to hear from you about your single life and adventures! Do let me know by mail or email (GGalice@GorgeousGrandma.com) which suggestions in this book you found helpful and may have caused even a slight change in your life.

Also, do visit **http://www.GorgeousGrandma.com** and sign up for HOT FLASHES, our popular email newsletter. Or, just drop in at the website and sign the Guest Book. Let's not lose touch with one another.

Warm thoughts,
Alice Solomon

APPENDIX B
EDUCATION VACATIONS

Elderhostel: (617) 426-7788. Offers thousands of trips a year for folks fifty-five and older, from birdwatching in Arizona to cultural tours of Peru, trekking in Nepal, or cruising to Newfoundland. Write for catalog: 75 Federal Street, Dept. M6, Boston, MA 02110-1941. On the Web: www.elderhostel.org

Explorations In Travel: (802)257-0152. Offers a selection of adventures for women over forty. Group travel programs featuring hiking and the outdoors. Call or visit website at www.exploretravel.com.

ElderTreks: (416) 588-5000. Worldwide cultural, nature, and adventure programs for those fifty and over. Based in Toronto.

Eye of the Whale: (808) 889-0227. Whale watching in Hawaii.

Family Hostel: (800) 733-9753. Administered by the University of New Hampshire. Offers escorted overseas tours for children ages eight to fifteen and their parents and/or grandparents. Accommodations are in family-friendly hotels.

Grandtravel: (800) 247-7651. Offers grandparent-grandchild trips, both in the United States and overseas. Based in Chevy Chase, Md.

Interhostel: (800) 733-9753. Administered by the University of New Hampshire. Offers overseas cultural tours in cooperation with universities and colleges, with most accommodations in university residence halls (to keep prices lower).

Saga Holidays: (617) 262-2262. Based in Boston. Longstanding travel company (Great Britain since 1952; United States since 1981). Operates tours for ages fifty and older. Known for its "Road Scholar" tours.

Seniors Abroad: (619) 485-1696 or write them at 12533 Pacato Circle N., San Diego, CA 92128. Not-for-profit international home-stay exchange program for ages fifty and over.

Seniors at Sea: (800) 453-9283. Escorted cruises on major cruise ships for people fifty and older, with shipboard classes. Based in Bothell, Washington.

Smithsonian Study Tours: (202) 357-4400. Study tours in United States and overseas.

University Vacations: (800) 792-0100. Vacation study programs in U.S. and Europe.

Appendix C
Travel Companion and Travel for Singles Agencies

All Singles Travel
1150 Lake Hearn Drive NE
Atlanta, GA 30342
(800) 717-3231
The company offers one land or cruise trip a month with twenty to thirty people aged thirty to sixty. Their trips typically run 40 percent men and 60 percent women.

Discount Travel Club
1083 North Collier Boulevard
Marco Island, FL 34145
(800) 393-5000
www.singlescruise.com
The company deals exclusively in singles' cruises. It organizes trips of one hundred to three hundred people ranging in ages from thirty to sixty, generally with an equal number of men and women.

O Solo Mio
160 Main Street
Los altos, CA 94022
(800) 959-8568
www.osolomio.com
This company offers about forty tours a year, each with twenty to forty-five participants ranging in age from mid-twenties to sixties. The ratio of men to women is usually about three to seven.

Saga Holidays
(800) 432 -1432
This big tour operator, specializing in older travelers, has a few "singles only" tours offered each year.

Singles Travel International
310 North State Street
Lockport, IL 60441
(877) 765-6874
www.singlestravelintl.com

The Women's Travel Club
21401 NE 38th Avenue
Aventura, FL 33180
(800) 480-4448
This club offers members a series of long and short trips. Single or shared accommodations are available, and men are invited to join some trips. Members get a monthly newsletter.

Travel Companions
Travel Companion Exchange
Box 833
Amityville, NY 11701
(800) 392-1256
This organization helps single travelers find compatible travel companions and roommates - same sex or opposite sex. Request a subscription to its newsletter.

Appendix D
Travel Newsletters

Consumer Reports Travel Letter
Box 53629
Boulder, CO 80322
(800) 234-1970
This newsletter provides tips, bargains, travel advisories, rankings, and ratings.

The Mature Traveler
PO Box 50400
Reno, NV 89513
(800) 460-6676
This publication offers travel discounts for people over fifty. Send a postcard for a free sample newsletter.

Solo Dining Savvy
PO Box 1025
So. Pasadena, CA 91031
(800) 299-1079
Ms. Alexander publishes news from restauranteurs about what they offer to attract solo diners. She urges single diners who have a bad restaurant experience to write to her.

Travel Companions
Travel Companion Exchange
Box 833
Amityville, NY 11701
(800) 392- 1256
This group helps single travelers find compatible travel companions and roommates — same sex or opposite sex. Sign up for its newsletter.

Travel Smart
50 Beechdale Road
Dobbs Ferry, NY 10522
(800) 327-3633
This newsletter offers agents' picks, travel deals, readers' tips, and new products.

APPENDIX E
CIVIC ORGANIZATIONS

Here are the national offices of local civic organizations:

International Association of Lions Clubs
300 22nd Street
Oak Brook, IL 60521-8842 (708) 571-5466

Kiwanis International
3636 Woodview Terrace
Indianapolis, IN 46268

**National Association of American Business Clubs
(AMBUCS)**
PO Box 5127
High Point, NC 27262

Rotary International
One Rotary Center
1560 Sherman Avenue
Evanston, IL 60201 (312) 866-3243

APPENDIX F
SPORTS ASSOCIATIONS

Each club's national office is listed below in case there is no local association in your city.

American Hiking Society
1015 31st Street NW
Washington, DC 20007-4490   (202) 385-3252

American Water Ski Association
799 Overlook Drive
Winter Haven, FL 33884 (813) 324-4341

Balloon Federation of America
PO Box 891
King of Prussia, PA 19406

International Windsurfers Class Association
2030 East Gladwick Street
Compton, CA 90220   (213) 608-1651

National Horseshoe Pitchers Association
Box 278
Munroe Falls, OH 44262

National Organization for River Sports
314 North 20th Street
Box 6847
Colorado Springs, CO 80904 (719) 473-2466

U.S. Amateur Confederation of Roller Skating
PO Box 6579
Lincoln, NE 68506 (402) 483-7551

U. S. Badminton Association
501 West Sixth Street
Papillion, NE 68046 (402) 592-7309

U.S. Croquet Association
500 Avenue of Champions
Palm Beach, FL 33418   (407) 627-3999

U.S. Curling Association
1100 Center Point Drive, Box 971
Stevens Point, WI 54481 (715) 344-1199

U.S. Cycling Federation
1750 East Boulder Street
Colorado Springs, CO 80909-5774

U.S. Diving Association
Pan American Plaza
201 South Capitol Avenue
Indianapolis, IN 46225

U.S. Fencing Association
1750 East Boulder Street
Colorado Springs, CO 80909-5774

U.S. Figure Skating Association
20 First Street
Colorado Springs, CO 80906 (719) 635-5200

U.S. Golf Association
Golf House
PO Box 708
Far Hills, NJ 07931-00708   (800) 223-0041

U.S. Hang Gliding Association
PO Box 8300
Colorado Springs, CO 80933 (719) 632-8300

U.S. Paddle Tennis Association
PO Box 30
Culver City, CA 90232

U.S. Polo Association
4059 Iron Works Pike
Lexington, KY 40511 (606) 255-0593

U.S. Ski Association
PO Box 100
Park City, UT 84060 (801) 649-9090

U.S. Table Tennis Association
1750 East Boulder Street
Colorado Springs, CO 80909 (719) 578-4583

U.S. Water Polo, Inc.
1780 East Boulder Street
Colorado Springs, CO 80909

U.S. Yacht Racing Association
Box 209
Newport, RI 02840 (401) 849-5200

APPENDIX G
ADVENTURE CAMPS AND ORGANIZATIONS

Call for information and to request a brochure.

American Wilderness Experience
PO Box 1486
Boulder, CO 80306
(800) 444-0099

Earthwatch
680 Mt. Auburn Street
Box 403
Watertown, MA 02172
(617) 926-8200

Foundation for Field Research
PO Box 2010
Alpine, CA 92001-0020
(619) 445-9264

Outward Bound USA
384 Field Point Road
Greenwich, CT 06830
(800) 243-8520

Sierra Club
730 Polk Street
San Francisco, CA 94019
(415) 776-2211

RECOMMENDED READING

For your interest, I have compiled a number of sources listed on the following pages which I hope will assist you to enhance your single life as well as help you find the love of your life. A number of these books were used in my research while others are appealing because of their subject matter.

The books are categorized in the following manner:

* Celebrating Life After Fifty

* Recovering From Loss

* Health, Wellness, and Image

* Meeting Men

* Personal Ads and On-Line Dating

* Relationships

* Sex and Sexuality

* Traveling Solo

* Living Together and Marrying Again

CELEBRATING LIFE AFTER FIFTY:

Brehony, Kathleen A. *Awaking at Midlife*, New York: Riverhead Books, 1996.

Brown, Helen Gurley. *The Late Show: A Semiwild But Practical Survival Plan for Women Over Fifty.* New York: William Morrow, 1993.

Downes, Peggy, Ph.D. and Faul, Patricia and Mud, Virginia and Tuttle, Ilene. *The New Older Woman: A Dialogue for the Coming Century.* Berkeley, CA: Celestial Arts, 1996.

Friedan, Betty. *The Fountain of Age.* New York: Simon and Schuster, 1993.

Jacobs, Ruth Harriet. *Be an Outrageous Older Woman - A R*A*S*P* Remarkable Aging Smart Person.* Manchester, CT: KIT, 1991.

Porcino, Jane. *Growing Older, Getting Better. A Handbook for Women in the Second Half of Life.* Reading, MA: Addison-Wesley, 1983.

Sheehy, Gail. *New Passages: Mapping Your Life Across Time.* New York: Random House, 1995.

Sher, Barbara. *It's Only Too Late if You Don't Start Now; How to Create Your Age.* New York: Delacorte Press, 1999.

Viorst, Judith. *Forever Fifty and Other Negotiations.* New York: Simon & Schuster, 1989.

Viorst, Judith. *Suddenly 60: And Other Shocks of Later Life.* New York: Simon & Schuster, 2000.

Weaver, Frances. *The Girls With the Grandmother Faces: A Celebration of Life's Potential for Those Over 55.* New York: Hyperion, 1996.

Recovering From Loss:

Bernstein, Judith R. *When the Bough Breaks: Forever After the Death of a Son or Daughter.* New York: Andrews McMeel Publishing, 1998.

Ford, Debbie, et al. *Spiritual Divorce: Divorce as a Catalyst for an Extraordinary Life.* San Francisco, CA: Harper, 2001.

Hannon, Kerry. *Suddenly Single: Money Skills for Divorcees and Widows.* New York: John Wiley & Sons, 1998.

Hayes, Christopher L. Ph.D. et al. *Our Turn: Women Who Triumph in the Face of Divorce.* New York: John Wiley & Sons, 1998.

James, John W. *The Grief Recovery Handbook.* New York: HarperCollins, 1999.

Jaycox, Victoria. *Single Again: A Guide For Women Starting Over.* New York: W.W. Norton, 1999.

Kaganoff, Penny (ed.), Spano, Susan (ed.), Austin-Smith, Vicki (ed.). *Women on Divorce: A Bedside Companion.* New York: Harcourt Brace, 1992.

Kahn, Sandra S. *Leaving Him Behind: Cutting the Cord and Breaking Free After the Marriage Ends.* New York: Random House, 1992.

Kushner, Harold S. *When Bad Things Happen to Good People.* New York: Schocken Books, 1981.

Loewinsohn, Ruth Jean. *Survival Handbook for Widows.* Chicago: Follett, 1979.

Lord, Janice Harris. *No Time for Goodbyes: Coping With Sorrow, Anger, and Injustice.* Los Angeles, CA: Pathfinder, 2001.

Noel, Brook and Blair, Pamela D. *I Wasn't Ready to Say Goodbye: Surviving, Coping, and Healing After the Sudden Death of a Loved One.* New York: Champion, 2001.

Steinem, Gloria. *Revolution From Within: A Book of Self-Esteem*. Boston, MA: Little, Brown, 1993.

Trafford, Abigail. *Crazy Time: Surviving Divorce and Building a New Life*. New York: HarperPerennial, 1992.

Wallerstein, Judith and Blakeslee, Sandra. *Second Chances*. New York: Ticknor and Fields, 1989.

Yates, Martha. *Coping: A Survival Manual for Women Alone*. Englewood Cliffs, NJ: Prentice-Hall, 1976.

FLIRTING:

Jillson, Joyce. *The Fine Art Of Flirting*. New York: Simon and Schuster, 1989.

Rabin, Susan, with Barbara Lagowski. *How to Attract Anyone, Anytime, Anyplace: The Smart Guide to Flirting*. New York: Plume, 1993.

Rabin, Susan, with Barbara Lagowski. *101 Ways to Flirt: How to Get More Dates and Meet Your Mate*. New York: Plume, 1997.

HEALTH, WELLNESS, AND IMAGE:

The Boston Women's Health Book Collective. *The New Our Bodies, Ourselves for the New Century*. Boston, MA: Touchstone Books, 1998.

Bransford, Helen. *Welcome to Your Facelift*. New York: Doubleday, 1997.

Busch, Julia. *Treat Your Face Like a Salad!* Coral Gables, FL: Anti-Aging Books, 1993.

Carper, Jean. *Stop Aging Now! The Ultimate Plan for Staying Young and Reversing the Aging Process*. New York: HarperPerennial, 1996.

Sheehy, Gail. *The Silent Passage: Menopause.* New York: Random House, 1991.

Stover, Laren et al. *The Bombshell Manual of Style.* New York: Hyperion, 2001.

MEETING MEN:

Blake, Tom. *Single Again: Dating and Meeting New Friends the Second Time Around.* Holbrook, MA: Adams Media, 2000.

Courtney, Phillipa. *4 Steps to Bring the Right Person Into Your Life Right Now!* New York: Meant2BeUnlimited, 2000.

French, Harold Stanley. *Dating and Mating for the Woman Over 50.* New York: New Century Publishing, 1999.

Gray, John. *Mars and Venus Starting Over.* New York: HarperCollins, 1998.

Lederman, Ellen. *The Best Places to Go to Meet Good Men.* Rocklin, CA: Prima Publishing, 1991.

Lownes, Leil. *How to Make Anyone Fall in Love With You.* New York: Contemporary Books, 1996.

Sanford, Teddi, and Mickie Padorr Silverstein. *Marrying Again: The Art of Attracting a New Man and Winning His Heart.* New York: Contemporary Books, 1998.

Tessina, Tina. *The Unofficial Guide to Dating Again.* New York: IDG Books, 1999.

Tucker, Nita, et al. *How Not to Stay Single.* New York: Crown Pub., 1996.

Wingo, John, and Julia Wingo. *At Long Last Love.* New York: Warner Books, 1994.

Wolf, Sharon. *Guerrilla Dating Tactics: Strategies, Tips and Secrets for Finding Romance.* New York: Penguin Books, 1993.

Wolf, Sharon, and Katy Koontz. *50 Ways to Find a Lover*. Holbrook, MA: Bob Adams, 1992.

Zuckerman, Rachelle. *Young at Heart: The Mature Woman's Guide to Finding and Keeping Romance*. New York: McGraw-Hill, 2001.

Personal Ads and On-Line Dating:

Booth, Richard, and Marshall Jung. *Romancing the Net: A "Tell-All" Guide to Love Online*. Rocklin, CA: Prima Publishing, 1996.

Calvo, Emily Thornton, and Laurence Minsky. *25 Words or Less: How to Write Like a Pro to Find That Special Someone Through Personal Ads*. New York: NTC/Contemporary Publishing, 1998.

Harrison, Barbara. *50+ and Looking for Love Online*. New York: Crossing Press, 2000.

Rabin, Susan, with Barbara Lagowski. *Cyberflirt: How to Attract Anyone, Anytime on the World Wide Web*. New York: Plume, 2000.

Skirloff, Lisa, and Jodie Gould. *Men Are From Cyberspace: The Single Woman's Guide to Flirting, Dating and Finding Love Online*. New York: St. Martin's Griffin, 1999.

Relationships:

Brothers, Joyce. *What Every Woman Should Know About Men*. New York: Ballantine Books, 1983.

Carter, Steven, and Julia Sokol. *What Smart Women Know*. New York: M. Evan & Co., 2000.

Cowan, Connell and Melvyn Kinder. *Smart Women/Foolish Choices: Finding the Right Man/Avoiding the Wrong Ones*. New York: New American Library, 1988.

Cowan, Connell and Melvyn Kinder. *Women Men Love/ Women Men Leave.* New York: New American Library, 1988.

DeAngelis, Barbara. *Secrets About Men Every Woman Should Know.* New York: Dell Publishing, 1992.

Gray, John. *Mars and Venus Starting Over.* New York: HarperCollins, 1998.

Page, Susan. *If I'm So Wonderful, Why Am I Still Single?* New York: Viking Penguin, 1988.

Shapiro, Susan R., and Michele Kasson. *The Men Out There: A Woman's Little Black Book.* Bethel, CT: Rutledge Books, 1997.

Sills, Judith. *How to Stop Looking for Someone Perfect and Find Someone to Love.* New York: Ballantine Books, 1984.

SEX AND SEXUALITY:

Barbach, Lonnie, Ph. D. *For Each Other: Sharing Sexual Intimacy.* New York: Penguin Books, 1984.

Barbach, Lonnie. *For Yourself.* New York: Doubleday, 1976.

Block, Joel, and Susan Crain Bakos. *Sex Over 50.* West Nyack, NY: Parker Publishing, 1999.

Boteach, Shmuley. *Kosher Sex: A Recipe for Passion and Intimacy.* New York: Doubleday, 2000.

Gray, John. *Mars and Venus in the Bedroom.* New York: HarperCollins, 1995.

Keesley, Barbara. *All Night Long: How to Make Love to a Man Over 50.* New York: HarperCollins, 2000.

Masterson, Graham. *How to Drive Your Man Wild in Bed.* New York: Penguin Books, 1976.

TRAVELING SOLO:

(See Appendix B for Travel Newsletters)

Ben-Lesser, Jay. *A Foxy Old Woman's Guide to Traveling Alone: Around Town or Around the World.* New York: Crossing Press, 1995.

Berman, Eleanor. *Traveling Solo: Advice and Ideas for More Than 250 Great Vacations.* Old Saybrook, CT: The Globe Pequot Press, 1999.

Bond, Marybeth. *Travelers' Tales: Gutsy Women, Travel Tips and Wisdom for the Road.* New York: Travelers' Tales, 1995.

Greenberg, Peter. *The Travel Detective: How to Get the Best Service and Best Deals for Airlines, Hotels, Cruise Ships, and Car Rental Agencies.* New York: Random House, 2001.

Heilman, Joan Rattner. *Unbelievably Good Deals and Great Adventures That You Absolutely Can't Get Unless You're Over 50.* Chicago: Contemporary Books, 1996.

McMillon, Bill. *Volunteer Vacations.* Chicago, IL: Chicago Review Press, 1997.

Wingler, Sharon. *Travel Alone and Love It: A Flight Attendant's Guide to Solo Travel.* Evanston, IL: Chicago Spectrum Press, 1996.

Zepatos, Thalia. *A Journey of One's Own: Uncommon Advice for the Independent Woman Traveler.* Portland, OR: Eighth Mountain Press, 1996.

LIVING TOGETHER AND MARRYING AGAIN:

Engel, Marjorie, et al. *Weddings, A Family Affair: The New Etiquette for Second Marriages and Couples With Divorced Parents.* New York: Wilshire Publishing, 1998.

Moseley, Douglas, et al. *Making Your Second Marriage a First Class Success.* Rocklin, CA: Prima Publishing, 1998.

Warner, Ralph, et al. *Living Together: A Legal Guide for Unmarried Couples*. New York: Nolo Press, 2001.

Wright, H. Norman. *Before You Remarry*. New York: Harvest House Press, 1999.

BIBLIOGRAPHY

Anderson, Carol M., and Susan Steward with Sonia Dimidjian. *Flying Solo: Single Women in Midlife.* New York: W.W. Norton & Company, 1994, p. 81, pp. 193-200.

Angier, Natalie. "Men, Women, Sex & Darwin", *New York Times Magazine*, February 21, 1999, p.50.

Brothers, Joyce, Ph.D. *What Every Woman Should Know About Men.* New York: Ballantine Books, 1983.

Carroll, Diahann: "Don't Date Married Men", *Star*, Sept. 18, 2001, p. 34.

DeAngelis, Barbara, Ph.D. *How To Make Love All The Time.* New York: Macmillan Publishing Co., 1987, p. 76.

Estrich, Susan. *Making the Case for Yourself: A Diet Book for Smart Women.* New York: Riverhead Books, 1998.

Friedan, Betty. *The Fountain of Age.* New York: Simon and Schuster, 1993.

Janda, Louis Ph.D. *Love & Sex Tests.* Adams Media, Holbrook, MA, 1998, p. 4.

Jillson, Joyce. *The Fine Art of Flirting.* New York: Simon & Schuster, 1984. p. 167.

Jong, Erica. *Fear of Fifty.* New York: HarperCollins, 1994.

Kelley, Susan Curtin. *Why Men Commit.* Holbrook, MA: Bob Adams, Inc.,1991.

Lederman, Ellen. *The Best Places to Meet Good Men.* Rocklin, CA: Prima Publishing, 1991.

Lowndes, Leil. *How to Make Anyone Fall in Love With You.* Chicago, IL: Contemporary Books, 1996, p. 89.

"Are You Aging Gracefully?" *Longevity Magazine*, Oct. 1994, p. 92

"The New Middle Age." *Newsweek,* December 7, 1992.

Peach, Dana, *DateSmart Quiz.* www.thirdage/com/features/love/datesmart/essentials

Scheele, Dr. Adele, "Coping With Ageism." *Working Woman,* February 1994.

Sheehy, Gail. *New Passages: Mapping Your Life Across Time.* New York: Random House, 1995.

Sheehy, Gail. *Understanding Men's Passages.* New York: Random House, 1998.

Skriloff, Lisa and Gould, Jodie. *Men Are From Cyberspace: The Single Woman's Guide to Flirting, Dating and Finding Love On-line.* New York: St. Martin's Griffin, 1996.

20/20 , the television segment that aired September 18, 1998.

"The Changing Lifestyles of Older People." *U.S. News and World Report,* September 18, 1995.

Viorst, Judith. *Necessary Losses.* New York: Ballantine Books, 1993.

Wolf, Sharon. *Guerilla Dating Tactics: Strategies, Tips and Secrets for Finding Romance.* New York: Penguin Books, 1993.

Wolf, Sharon and Koontz, Katy. *50 Ways to Find a Lover.* Holbrook, MA: Bob Adams, 1992.

INDEX

About the Author

Alice Solomon reentered the working world after her graduation from Wellesley College cum laude at the age of fifty. She has held a number of marketing, public relations, sales, fashion, and promotional roles within business and non-profit organizations. Alice was chosen to be the subject of a feature article in Ms. magazine on women who reenter the workplace.

From 1994 to 2001, Alice was a syndicated newspaper columnist, writing "A Guide for Gorgeous Grandmas" for the *MetroWest Daily News*, in Framingham, Massachusetts, and other newspapers in Massachusetts and Florida, with a readership of over 150,000. She hosted twice-weekly radio shows on WXKS-FM in Wellesley, Massachusetts, while enjoying guest appearances on other radio shows and television programs as well. In 2002, Alice was heard in Palm Beach County on radio station WPBI-AM as co-host of the daily show "Upbeat Senior Magazine on the Air."

Involved in community service throughout her life, Alice chaired or sat on the board of directors of the Framingham Union Hospital, the United Way, the United Jewish Appeal, the National Council of Jewish Women, the Massachusetts Easter Seal Society, and the National Head Injury Foundation.

Alice's first book was *Advice From a Gorgeous Grandma: For Single Women Over Fifty Who Want to Survive, Thrive, Live, Love, Date, Mate, and Have a Ball!* Her magazine articles were featured in *Upbeat Senior Magazine,* and her website, http://www.GorgeousGrandma.com, received the Golden Web Award 2002-2003.

Gorgeous Grandma Communications, Alice's public speaking and advisory service, was selected by the Small Business Development Center at Florida Atlantic University as a Potential Business Success. Alice has appeared as guest speaker for numerous clubs and organizations.

Alice held the titles of Mrs. Massachusetts and Mrs. U.S. Savings Bonds for Massachusetts, and her family was selected the Massachusetts All-American Family, encompassing representation of both the U.S. Treasury Department and the Commonwealth of Massachusetts. During that reign, she addressed the Massachusetts Senate and the Massachusetts House of Representatives on the subjects of family values and community service.

Alice lives currently in Delray Beach, Florida, and she is the proud grandmother of five gorgeous (of course) grandchildren.

What others* are saying about
http://www.GorgeousGrandma.com

"Fantastic idea! I've been advocating the need for sites where 50ish women, single and otherwise can chat, discuss, argue and philosophize with people just like US! Who speak OUR language, share our views, come from the same time period of life. Bravo to your ideas, and I look forward to seeing more about it as this all develops. Thanks for making the seeds germinate!" *- Donna*

"What a great website! From a GG in Sydney Australia, well done. I am the mother of 2, divorced, and loving the freedom. Have so much to do, so many people to meet, and so many places to see. I intend to make every moment count. Seems to me that's what this site is all about. More power to you all, ladies." *- Doreen*

"Hey! I'm gorgeous, a grandma of two stunning babies, I love the life I live after working out that I'm not anybody's doormat. I'm three quarters through a double degree at university, and I've survived two bad marriages, drug and alcohol addiction, and a nightmare childhood. I'd say that I am most definitely eligible for Gorgeous Grandmas, wouldn't you? Problem is, I'm only 42 - could I be an honourable GG? Love and lots of respect for what you're doing - (more power to us!)" *- Val*

"Hi! I just found your site and think it is wonderful that someone is out there for all the GGs in the world. I have just recently left my job and moved across country to finally be close to my grandkids and I am loving every minute of it. Finding your site has made my day. Thank you for remembering us all." *- Martha*

"Hi GG!! Love your site. I am a class of '52 mother of 12 children (3 girls & 9 boys). I have always tried to keep looking and thinking young. I consider myself a GG as well. I have 17 grandchildren & 2 on the way as well as 1 just born great grandchild. I am retired from sales. Keep us on the GG track. You go girl!!!!" *- Joan*

"Fantastic to find this. Mother of 4 Granny of 8. Retired ATC AFSS Spec. and now I manage a weather observer site. Love to dig in my garden, travel, dance, movies, just about anything. Favorite vacation spot, Las Vegas. I hope to be an very active person as long as I live. Thanks..."
- Madeline

"Kudos, Alice. I happened upon your page as I was searching for a 50's chat room. Lucky find! It's a great idea. Sometimes I feel like the odd one because I don't act the way others think grandmas are supposed to act. I'm a competitive tennis player, great lover of music and love to dance! Stay in touch!"
- JoAnne

"I'm so glad to see this. I work about 50 hours a week, own my own home and have raised 4 kids pretty much by myself. I was my husband's wife, my kids' mother and now a grandmother but seldom does a woman get recognized as a person with a mind and ideas. I'm enjoying my freedom, my house is decorated Victorian style which my husband would have hated, which makes me like it even more. I don't want to find a man to make me happy. I like making my own decisions and choices. Keep up the good work."
- Sheila

"Hello, hello. My daughter found your website and forwarded it to me. It looks like a great delight. I work full time, widowed for several years, kids all on their own and wanting to add some variety to my life. Thank you to whoever put this site in motion."
-Marlene

"Wonderful idea! Just came by your website by accident. I'm fifty-seven, but look and feel much younger. I'm not a grandma yet but hope to be one of these days! For now my pets are my grandkids. I was widowed after 33 years of marriage to my high school sweetheart."
- Bonnie

"What a very beautiful and informative site. You make me envious of the great job you have done. Keep up the great work."
- Irene

"I loved you site. I always say 50 is just the beginning of life. Now we have the experience to enjoy all we have learned and yet have a whole new world at our feet"
- Louisa

"So glad to know there are others like me. I've raised 4 children and have 2 wonderful grandchildren. Becoming single and a senior has been a shock but I'm not giving in to the rocking chair yet. I winter in Florida and have discoved seniors have a lot of power and can be beach bums, fisherwomen, or be glamorous and travel. It's fun to put on a different hat and let all the secret me's out."
- Helen

Read these and other comments on the "Sign the Guestbook" page at http://www.GorgeousGrandma.com.